#30-2001   BR Bid   June 2002

NORTH CAROLINA
STATE BOARD OF COMMUNITY COLLEGES
LIBRARIES
SOUTHEASTERN COMMUNITY COLLEGE

PLAN SMART,
RETIRE RICH

SOUTHEASTERN COMMUNITY
COLLEGE LIBRARY
WHITEVILLE, NC 28472

HG
179
.P5552
1999

PLAN SMART, RETIRE RICH

The Book Designed to Help You Reach Your Retirement Dreams

SOUTHEASTERN COMMUNITY
COLLEGE LIBRARY
WHITEVILLE, NC 28472

**GEORGE D. BRENNER, JD, CLU, CHFC
STEPHEN ABRAMSON, CLU, CHFC, CPC
BARRY L. RABINOVICH, JD, AEP
STANFIELD HILL, JD, CLU
STEVEN K. RABINAW**

Co-published with MONY Life Insurance Company, a subisidiary of The MONY Group, Inc. (NYSE: MNY). MONY Life Insurance Company is a New York-domiciled life insurer that was founded in 1842 as The Mutual Life Insurance Company of New York. The Mutual Life Insurance Company of New York underwrote the first mutual life insurance policy in the United States in 1843. In 1998, The Mutual Life Insurance Company of New York converted to a stock company through demutualization and was renamed MONY Life Insurance Company. The MONY name reflects the company's heritage.

McGraw-Hill

New York   San Francisco   Washington, D.C.   Auckland   Bogotá
Caracas   Lisbon   London   Madrid   Mexico City   Milan
Montreal   New Delhi   Singapore
Sydney   Tokyo   Toronto

Library of Congress Cataloging-in-Publication Data

Plan smart--retire rich : the book designed to help you reach your
  retirement dreams / The Mutual Life Insurance Company of New York.
    p. cm.
  ISBN 0-07-044464-1
    1. Retirement income--Planning. I. Mutual Life Insurance Company
of New York.
  HG179.P5552 1998
  332.024'01—dc21   98-41404
                                                                        CIP

McGraw-Hill
A Division of The McGraw-Hill Companies

Copyright © 1999 by The Mutual Life Insurance Company of New York. All rights
reserved. Printed in the United States of America. Except as permitted under the
United States Copyright Act of 1976, no part of this publication may be reproduced,
transmitted, or distributed in any form or by any means, or stored in a data base or
retrieval system, electronic, mechanical, photocopying, recording or otherwise, without
the prior written permission of the publisher and the copyright holder.

1 2 3 4 5 6 7 8 9 0 DOC/DOC 9 0 3 2 1 0 9 8

ISBN 0-07-044464-1

The sponsoring editor for this book was Jeffrey Krames, the editing supervisor was
Donna Muscatello, and the production supervisor was Suzanne W. B. Rapcavage. It was
typeset in 11/13 New Century Schoolbook by Lisa King of Editorial and Production
Services.

Printed and bound by R. R. Donnelley & Sons Company.

This publication is designed to provide accurate and authoritative information in
regard to the subject matter covered. It is sold with the understanding that the author
nor the publisher is engaged in rendering legal, accounting, futures/securities trading,
or other professional service. If legal advice or other expert assistance is required, the
services of a competent professional person should be sought.

—From a Declaration of Principles jointly adopted by a Committee of the
American Bar Association and a Committee of Publishers.

McGraw-Hill books are available at special quantity discounts to use as premiums and
sales promotions, or for use in corporate training programs. For more information,
please write to the Director of Special Sales, McGraw-Hill, 11 West 19th Street, New
York, NY 10011. Or contact your local bookstore.

 This book is printed on recycled, acid-free paper containing a minimum
of 50% recycled de-inked fiber.

CONTENTS

Introduction   ix

Profiles   xiii

Acknowledgments   xvii

PART ONE

Chapter 1

Retirement 101: Learning the Basics   3
Understanding the basic financial and retirement concepts necessary for developing an effective retirement program for you.

Chapter 2

Financial Architecture: Creating a Portfolio Blueprint   13
Understanding risk and asset allocation.

Chapter 3

Learn from the Past: Avoid Mistakes in the Future   27
A list of common retirement errors that anyone can make—and how to avoid them.

PART TWO

Chapter 4

Special (k): Using Your Employer's 401(k) Plan to Meet Your Retirement Goals   35
The advantages of participating in your 401(k) plan.

Chapter 5

Special (k): Adopting a 401(k) Plan to Meet Your Company's Needs   47
The business advantages of creating a 401(k) plan.

Chapter 6

Go with the Cash Flow: Profit-Sharing Plans   51

An answer for business owners who may want flexibility in plan contribution amount.

Chapter 7

Two for Your Money: Combining Defined Contribution Plans   59

An option offering maximum opportunity and flexibility for the business owner in need of higher contributions and minimum commitments.

Chapter 8

Supercharging Your Retirement Program: A Plan for Late Starters and Those over Fifty   67

Using a defined benefit plan to help older and wealthier business owners maximize their contributions.

Chapter 9

The Age of Reason Begins: Older Can Be Better   73

The age-based profit-sharing plan for those employers who are older than their employees and who want flexibility in plan contribution amount.

Chapter 10

Simply the Best— The Ins and Outs of the SIMPLE Plan   77

Understanding a new type of retirement plan tailor-made for certain business owners.

Chapter 11

Closing the Gap: What To Do When Your Employer's Plan Just Isn't Enough   81

How to take control of your retirement by using tax-favored products to help supplement your retirement plan.

PART THREE

Chapter 12

The Midas Touch: Doing the Impossible with Creative Business Strategies   93

Five case studies for the successful business owner which show how to lower taxes and/or increase retirement benefits.

Chapter 13

Give and Ye Shall Receive: The Benefits of Rewarding Key Employees   103

The advantages of setting up a discriminatory retirement program designed for key employees.

Chapter 14

Planning for Keeps: How to Keep Together What You Put Together   119

Minimizing estate and income taxes for individuals with substantial retirement accounts.

Chapter 15

Double Your Advantage: Use Your Retirement Plan to Help Protect Your Estate   139

Using tax deductible contributions to pay premiums for life insurance that is needed for estate planning.

Chapter 16

You Can't Take It with You: Business Succession Planning   155

Using a qualified plan to help fund a business continuation program.

Chapter 17

To Have and to Hold: Medicaid Asset Protection   163

Protecting property from Medicaid recapture.

Chapter 18

The Honeymoon Is Over   185

Using a qualified plan account to fund marital obligations pursuant to divorce.

Chapter 19

Heads I Win, Tails I Win: Charitable Giving—Advantages for Both You and Your Favorite Charity   191

A creative way to use a charitable remainder trust as a retirement program.

Appendix A: A Spectrum of Retirement Plans   200

A summary of qualified retirement plans and their key attributes.

Appendix B: Summary of Recent Legislation   205

The effects of new legislation on your retirement plan.

Appendix C: Glossary of Financial Terms   215

Index   221

INTRODUCTION

A secure and comfortable retirement... for people of all generations, this is a universal goal. The ability to spend the post-career years in comfort and with dignity, to devote time to family, travel, and personal interests, can be the crowning chapter of a full and rich life.

Some questions to answer are:

1. Will you have the financial resources to make the dream come true?
2. How can you leverage your assets?
3. How can you protect what you accumulate during your working years and at retirement?
4. How can you minimize taxes?
5. How can you avoid outliving your income?

The answers depend to a great extent on how well you plan for retirement and for all of the contingencies that may occur. The more you allocate to building a retirement nest egg and the smarter you are in structuring your financial vehicles and the strategies designed to achieve your goals, the more likely you'll be able to retire to a lifestyle that matches or exceeds your expectations.

A wide range of retirement plans and techniques—some relatively simple, others complex and sophisticated—can provide powerful tax and financial advantages designed to leverage the power of your assets. Chances are you know this, but you may be confused as to which plans are best suited for your personal needs and circumstances. Some commonly asked questions are:

*   Should I contribute to an IRA?
*   Which one—a traditional IRA or the new Roth IRA (created by the 1997 Tax Act)?
*   Is a defined benefit plan better than a defined contribution plan?

- Can an employer establish a retirement program just for key people?
- How can highly appreciated property be sold without paying capital gains tax?
- Once I decide on the right plan or program, should I fund it with cash, stocks, annuities, or life insurance?

Accumulating money for retirement may be only half the battle. Once there, what's the best way to distribute money from a plan? How can you protect your money from taxes or creditors? What's the best way to pass it on to your children? What happens if you need nursing home care? Even if you are knowledgeable about finances and planning, you can fall into tax and financial traps or fail to take advantage of new opportunities created by Congress.

Sometimes, it seems you need a team of professionals to help you identify the key issues and make the right decisions.

That's precisely the idea behind *Plan Smart, Retire Rich.* Authored by experienced and knowledgeable professionals who help people and businesses sort out the issues and make the right decisions, *Plan Smart, Retire Rich* takes the mystery out of retirement planning and delivers powerful information keyed to your personal needs, goals, and financial resources. This book is divided into 19 chapters. To make the best use of the book, check the profile section beginning on page xii and identify the people most closely related to your personal situation. Whether you are a young or older business owner or executive, or retired, you will find someone like you in the profile section. Then turn to the appropriate chapters and you'll find detailed recommendations and compelling case studies that will illuminate the options and help guide you with exceptional accuracy.

To make the profile section easier to use, it is divided into four sections, as follows:

1. Section I shows important financial, tax, and retirement information which everyone should know.

2. Section II describes numerous strategies used by individuals and business owners to help plan for a successful retirement.

3.   Section III describes creative uses of retirement plans other than just funding benefits, along with ways to help protect property.

4.   Section IV contains appendixes—a summary of (1) the different types of qualified retirement plans and (2) recent legislation. There is also a glossary of terms.

To help fulfill your dreams and protect them, the *Plan Smart, Retire Rich* process is as follows:

1.   Look for profiles that are similar to your circumstances.

2.   Identify the strategies and tactics suggested by the authors.

3.   Implement the program that is most likely designed to achieve your goals.

4.   Avoid mistakes and traps.

5.   Make certain to review all aspects of your program with your legal, tax, and financial advisor(s).

Authors' Note: There are many financial strategies described in *Plan Smart, Retire Rich*. Some of these strategies are complex, while others are simple. We strongly urge the reader to consult with his or her own advisor before implementing any of them. The reasons for this are (1) we can't anticipate every contingency that could affect your retirement strategy; (2) laws change rapidly; and (3) we are not providing legal or tax advice to the reader.

PROFILES

HOW TO USE THIS BOOK

Plan Smart, Retire Rich utilizes "profiles," which are descriptions of people in different stages of life. We realize that young employees may have needs and goals different from older employees, and business owners have their own special needs. The purpose of profiles is to help you harness the knowledge of the experts by quickly identifying with one or more individuals described in the chapter. All you have to do is turn to the next page and quickly scan the chapter titles, the description of each chapter, and the type of person to whom the chapter applies. Some retirement concepts are universal and may apply to everyone. Other chapters may only apply to you. We have indicated which chapters should be read by whom.

Here are two examples of how profiles may work. Suppose you are a young executive or professional working for a company that has established a 401(k) plan. Since you do not own or control your company, you may not be interested in the chapters devoted to business owners. But you will be interested in the chapter on 401(k)s and several other retirement chapters applicable to you. If you are a business owner, you will be interested in those chapters describing smart retirement concepts for those who can design their own plans.

PROFILES

FOR WHOM	CHAPTER TITLE	DESCRIPTION	PAGE
Part One			
1. Everyone	Retirement 101: Learning the Basics	Understanding basic financial and retirement concepts necessary for developing the most effective retirement program for you	3

2.	Everyone	Financial Architecture: Creating a Portfolio Blueprint	What everyone should know about investing for retirement	13
3.	Everyone	Learn from the Past: Avoid Mistakes in the Future	A list of common retirement errors that anyone can make—and how to avoid them	27

Part Two

4.	Employees covered under a 401(k) plan	Special (k): Using Your Employer's 401(k) Plan to Meet Your Retirement Goals	The tax and financial advantages of participating in your 401(k) plan	35
5.	Employers setting up a 401(k) plan for their employees	Special (K): Adopting a 401(K) Plan to Meet Your Company's Needs	The tax and financial advantages of creating a 401(k) plan for employees	47
6.	Business owners who want to create a flexible retirement plan in which contributions can be changed each year or not made	Go with the Cash Flow: Profit-Sharing Plans	An answer for business owners who may want flexibility in plan contribution amount	51
7.	Profitable business owners with stable income who want to create a retirement plan in which some contributions are fixed	Two for Your Money: Combining Defined Contribution Plans	An option offering maximum opportunity and flexibility for the business owner in need of higher contributions and minimum commitments	59
8.	"Older" business owners who have higher income than other employees and who want to maximize contributions	Supercharging Your Retirement Program: A Plan for Late Starters and Those over Fifty	Using a defined benefit plan to help older and wealthier business owners maximize their contributions	67

9. For older employers who may want flexibility in plan contribution amount — The Age of Reason Begins: Older Can Be Better — The age-based profit-sharing plan for those employers who are older than their employees and who want flexibility in plan contribution amount — 73

10. Small business owners, especially those who operate their companies on a part-time basis — Simply the Best: The Ins and Outs of the SIMPLE Plan — A description of how a Simple IRA works for business owners — 77

11. Anyone who may need to accumulate additional retirement income over and above what his or her employer provides — Closing the Gap: What to Do When Your Employer's Plan Just Isn't Enough — Taking control of your retirement by using tax-favored products to help supplement your employer's plan — 81

Part Three

12. Successful business owners — The Midas Touch: Doing the Impossible with Creative Business Strategies — Five case studies that can reduce taxes and/ or increase retirement benefits for the successful business owner — 93

13. Business owners and key employees of a company — Give and You Shall Receive: The Benefits of Rewarding Key Employees — The advantages of setting up a discriminatory retirement program designed for key employees — 103

14. Any individual who has accumulated or will accumulate substantial retirement or IRA accounts — Planning for Keeps: How to Keep Together What You Put Together — Minimizing estate and income taxes for individuals with substantial retirement accounts — 119

15. Business owners who want to pay for life insurance premiums with income tax-deductible employer contributions — Double Your Advantage: Use Your Retirement Plan to Help Protect Your Estate — Using tax-deductible contributions to pay premiums for life insurance that is needed for estate planning — 139

16. Business owners who want to have their business continue after their death or retirement — You Can't Take It with You: Business Succession Planning — Using a qualified plan to help fund a business continuation program — 155

17.	Anyone who wants to protect his property or his parents' property from the high cost of nursing home care	To Have and To Hold: Medicaid Asset Protection	How to protect property from Medicaid recapture	163
18.	Anyone considering divorce who has a qualified plan account or IRA	The Honeymoon Is Over: Qualified Money and Divorce	A description of how qualified plan money or an IRA can be used to pay marital obligations	185
19.	Anyone who has accumulated appreciated capital property that may be needed for retirement	Heads I Win, Tails I Win: Charitable Giving— Advantages for Both You and Your Favorite Charity	A creative way to use a charitable remainder trust as a retirement program	191

APPENDIX

A.	Everyone	A Spectrum of Retirement Plans	A summary of the qualified retirement plans and their key attributes	200
B.	Everyone	Summary of Recent Legislation	The effects of new legislation on your retirement plan	205
C.	Everyone	Glossary of Financial Terms		215

ACKNOWLEDGMENTS

Plan Smart, Retire Rich could not have been written without substantial help of may individuals from MONY's Home Office. The writing of this book was truly a team effort. The authors would like to thank John Cecere, CLU, Vice President of Market Development and Implementation; Susan Delaney, JD, Director of Business and Estate Planning; Marilee Talley, CLU, Director of Seminar Development; and Bob Goldenberg, CLU, Assistant Vice President, Marketing Technology. Each of these professionals has years of experience in business and retirement planning, and has spent a significant amount of time helping the authors research, write, and organize the content of this book.

The authors would also like to thank David Waldman, Debra Silver, and Robert Levy from MONY's Law Department, and Terry Howe and Jose Gonzalez, Jr., from MONY's Compliance Department. Each of these professionals spent many hours reviewing the material for technical accuracy and to ensure that the content of the book satisfies all of MONY's high ethical and compliance standards.

Last, but certainly not least, we would like to thank Catherine Wolf, Rachel Lawson, and Cara Hughes, who were given the challenging task of typing the original manuscript several times, while coping with the demands of five authors, and helping us to organize our thoughts.

ONE

Part One describes important tax, financial, and retirement information everyone should know. In this section you will learn key retirement concepts, the financial pyramid, and how to avoid mistakes others have made when it comes to retirement planning.

Some of the key concepts are:

- The difference between defined contribution and defined benefit plans
- The power of compounding
- The role of life insurance
- How to calculate your retirement benefit
- The financial pyramid for asset diversification
- A list of financial traps to avoid

CHAPTER 1

Retirement 101: Learning the Basics

There is an old adage that says "numbers don't lie." So when it comes to figuring out how much you need or want for retirement, you need to understand basic math, a few retirement concepts, and some financial concepts. This is where you may wish you had paid more attention to your high school math teacher.

RETIREMENT CONCEPTS

There are three important retirement planning concepts, that everyone should be aware of. They are (1) defined benefit, (2) defined contribution, and (3) qualified versus nonqualified. A defined benefit plan provides for an individual to receive a specific income beginning at retirement. An example is a plan that provides an employee participant who retires at age 65 with a monthly benefit of $5,000, payable for life. That's the goal, or the defined benefit—you are certain of your future retirement benefit.

To reach your goal, you (or the employer funding the plan) need to calculate how much has to be saved each year. This amount depends upon four factors: (1) the fund value necessary to pay the benefit, (2) the number of years you have to save, (3) the interest you can earn on your money, and (4) the number of years the benefit will be paid.

Table 1-1 illustrates the amount you need to save annually to have a defined benefit of $5,000 per month based on your current age at two assumed interest rates.

This chart proves that numbers don't lie. If you want to attain your financial goal of having $5,000 per month for life starting at age 65, you need to save a specific amount annually. And the longer you wait to start, the more you have to set aside annually.

A defined contribution approach is the opposite of defined benefit. You don't know your retirement benefit but you do know your contribution. In other words, you plan to save or set aside a specific amount of money each year until your retirement. Your retirement benefit will be based on the future value of these contributions—which is unknown. Table 1-2 illustrates your future retirement accumulation at age 65, assuming you can save $5,000 annually.

Both tables illustrate one critical concept that can make a big difference in your retirement plan. Regardless of which approach you take, in general the best strategy is to *start early*. The earlier you start, the more you will have in a defined contribution plan, the larger your benefit will be in a defined benefit plan. And in a defined benefit plan, the later you start, the larger your contributions will have to be, because you have less time to reach your retirement goal.

TABLE 1-1

Annual Amount Needed to Provide $5,000/Month* at Age 65

Your Current Age	At 6%	At 8%
25	$ 4,100	$ 2,449
30	5,694	3,682
35	8,027	5,602
40	11,565	8,680
45	17,250	13,866
50	27,262	23,370
55	48,142	43,802

*1983 Individual Annuity Mortality table at 6% interest. In a qualified plan, the actual amount will be determined by the plan actuary.

TABLE 1-2

Future Value at Age 65

Your Current Age	At 5%	At 7%	At 9%
25	$634,199	$1,068,048	$1,841,459
30	474,182	739,562	1,175,624
35	348,804	505,365	742,876
40	250,567	338,382	461,620
45	173,596	219,326	160,017
50	113,287	134,440	160,012
55	66,034	73,918	82,801

One key to retiring with enough wealth is selecting the right type of plan. As you will learn in Part Two, there are many types of defined contribution plans. Profit sharing, money purchase, 401(k), SIMPLE, and IRAs are all types of defined contribution plans that are discussed.

The third concept to understand is qualified versus nonqualified plans. A qualified plan has to satisfy specific requirements of the law. Once the plan is qualified, certain tax and legal benefits are conferred upon the employer and plan participants. Among the most important are:

- Contributions (up to certain limits) are income tax deductible

- Interest or growth is income tax deferred

- Plans cannot discriminate in favor of "highly compensated employees"

- Plan accounts are generally exempt from claims of certain creditors

- Distributions can be rolled over to another plan or IRA

In contrast to qualified plans, businesses sometimes create nonqualified arrangements. These are retirement programs that are generally designed for one individual or one class of key employees. They can be used in addition to a qualified plan or in lieu of one. They can provide a specific retirement benefit just like a defined benefit plan, or provide that the employer or employee will set aside specific amounts each year as happens in a defined contribution plan. Nonqualified arrangements do not provide the same legal and tax benefits[1] as qualified plans, but they do have certain advantages. Among the most important are:

- The ability to decide who will and will not participate
- Ease and low or no cost of administration
- More flexibility in benefit structure

OTHER FACTORS TO CONSIDER

In developing a retirement plan there are several factors to consider in addition to the amount you need or want to save.

1. *Income Taxes.* The above discussion did not take into consideration income taxes. You might have to save more if you have to pay income taxes on all or part of your retirement benefit or your contributions. Distributions from qualified employer plans are always subject to income tax.

2. *Social Security.* You might want to consider social security benefits as part of your retirement. Eligible taxpayers can start to receive reduced benefits at age 62. These benefits can offset the amount you need to save.

3. *Inflation.* Inflation will erode the value of your money. Inflation is a fact of life. According to the government, inflation averaged 4 percent between 1957 and 1997. If you want to retire with the understanding that you can purchase goods and services in today's dollars, you should increase your retirement projection or goals by future increases in inflation. The impact of inflation can be illustrated in two ways. Let's assume your retirement goal is to accumulate $500,000 in 20 years and that inflation will average 4 percent per year. Your $500,000 will only equal $228,193 in today's buying power. If you want to accumulate $500,000 in today's value, you would have to accumulate $1,095,561 in the 20 years.

4. *Lifestyle.* When you retire, your lifestyle may change. If your goal is to sell your house, business, or any other asset and move into an apartment or smaller home, you should consider the net proceeds you may realize from the sale. If the proceeds

---

[1]No income tax deduction is realized until the benefit is paid to the employee.

from one or more of these assets are going to be used for retirement, you may have to save less each year.

You may also want to consider how you will spend money at retirement. Income needs may go down if you don't commute, do not have children to support, or move to a less expensive part of the country. However, decreases in costs may be offset by an increase in leisure time. You may spend more money on travel, entertainment, and health care (despite having medical insurance).

5. *Life Expectancy.* A conservative approach at retirement is to live off interest on money you accumulate. This prevents you from outliving your retirement income. There are two ways to do this. The first way is simply to invest your money and live off of the interest. If you have $500,000 and earn 6 percent interest, your income is $30,000. Your principal remains constant and can be invaded for emergencies or become a legacy for your family after your death.

A second approach is to use your retirement money to purchase an annuity from an insurance company. The annuity can pay you a guaranteed income as long as you live. This is called an *immediate life annuity.* If you want to provide a benefit for your spouse, you can purchase a *joint and survivor annuity*, which is payable over your life and your spouse's life. Guaranteed annuities at retirement are popular. They pay a fixed amount at a time when your income needs may remain constant. In exchange for your premium (your retirement accumulation), the insurance company pays you a promised benefit regardless of market conditions and regardless of how long you or your spouse lives. Fixed annuity payments do not increase. However, if you want your payment to increase, you may need a variable type of annuity or other financial product.

The disadvantages of purchasing pure life annuities are that you don't have access to your principal and you generally cannot leave a legacy for your family.[2] To illustrate, let's look at the following example. Suppose you purchase a joint and survivor annuity that pays you and your spouse an annuity of $5,000 per month as long as either of you lives. Once you purchase the annu-

---

[2]Generally, you can purchase an annuity that will pay a benefit for life but guarantee a certain number of payments if the annuitant dies before a specified period.

ity you don't have access to the principal (the cash you spent to pay for the annuity). However, your annuity payment is a combination of a return of your principal and interest. In essence, you are getting back your principal in monthly payments.

Both you and the insurance company assume risk when you purchase a pure life annuity. The risk you assume is that you won't live to life expectancy. The insurance company assumes the risk you will live past expectancy. If you die early, the insurance company makes money because the payout is less than expected. If you live past life expectancy, the insurance company loses money because the payout is greater than expected. So if you buy an annuity and want to "beat" the insurance company, remember what your mother told you: "Eat healthy, diet, and exercise."

6. *Use Common Sense*. When it comes to purchasing financial products or property or spending money, use the common sense you have accumulated during your life. At retirement, you might not be able to afford to lose money or become liable for losses. Remember another old adage: "If it is too good to be true, it's probably illegal." When in doubt, delay decisions and consult your advisor. Spending a few dollars on an attorney, accountant, or other advisor can save you money.

7. *Protect Against Disability*. Most people have to work to save money for retirement. If you are disabled because of illness or injury, you may lose your ability to save for retirement. To help protect against this contingency, you should have adequate disability income insurance. A disability policy can pay you a specific benefit if you are unable to work as defined in the policy.

Sometimes your employer may provide disability insurance through a group plan. Often, this insurance may not be adequate for your needs. You may want to supplement this benefit with your own policy. If you own your own business, it is critical to have overhead expenses and income protection. Without you, the business may cease to exist. Then there will be no one to pay your salary or business expenses.

8. *Protect Your Family After Death*. Your retirement plan provides benefits to you and may provide benefits to your spouse or another individual who is dependent upon you. If you die prior to retirement, your employer contributions and your contributions stop. In general, your beneficiary is only entitled to the accumulated value of your retirement account. This may not be enough to adequately support your beneficiary or to provide an adequate retirement for him or her.

Most employees who have families or other dependents need life insurance to help protect them. Without life insurance, the value of your assets may not be sufficient to provide adequate income for your beneficiary.

How much life insurance do you need and what type of insurance should you buy? These are difficult questions that you should discuss with your insurance professional. But there are some guidelines to follow:

- Don't assume you need an amount of life insurance that is simply equal to a multiple of your salary, such as 3, 4, or 5 times. You may need much more, or you may need less or none at all.

- Don't assume you no longer have insurance needs just because your children are grown or your spouse also works. A sixty-year-old surviving spouse may still have substantial income needs.

- Base your insurance on your financial needs and goals. If you want life insurance to replace lost income, you need a sum of money which generates income equal to the lost salary. Here's an example:

Harry and Sally are both 35 years old. Harry is a plant manager earning $65,000 annually. Sally is a full-time mother raising three children. If Harry dies, Sally determined she will need $55,000 of income to maintain her lifestyle. Sally assumes she can earn 7 percent on money. Between Harry's pension and their other assets, Sally will have an income of $20,000 if Harry dies. Thus, Sally needs to replace $35,000 of income. Assuming it's improbable for Sally to work because of the age of her children, she needs $500,000 of capital generating 7 percent interest to produce $35,000 of income (without invading principal). To replace income,* Harry should have $500,000 of life insurance on his life.

Even if Sally went back to work and could earn $35,000 annually, she still might need life insurance on Harry's life to help pay for childcare and other expenses.

---

*Income taxes and inflation have not been taken into consideration. Additional insurance may be needed to cover these expenses.

The type of life insurance you should buy depends on your needs. If your insurance need is long term, a cash value policy may be best. If your insurance need is temporary, then term insurance may be more appropriate. Long-term or temporary needs will vary based on your age and personal situation. Your insurance representative should be able to help you purchase the appropriate type of policy and the amount you need.

Regardless of the type and amount of life insurance, in this book you will learn creative ways to help you pay premiums.

9. *How To Calculate Your Retirement Benefit.* You need to know how to calculate your estimated retirement benefits based on your personal financial situation. To help you calculate this sum, the following is an easy-to-use retirement calculator with a case study.

RETIREMENT CALCULATOR

The following is a seven-step guide to help you determine if you are on target to meet your retirement goal, or how much you need to save annually to meet that goal.

	Amount
Step 1: Determine the amount of retirement income you desire and the retirement age you want it to begin. Most retirement advisors recommend you retire on about 70% of the income you earn during the year prior to retirement. On the other hand, many individuals desire to "better" their lifestyle at retirement and want to retire on 100% of their final year's income.	_____
Step 2: Determine your Social Security benefit at your retirement age. This benefit depends on your wages and the number of years you contributed to the Social Security system. The maximum benefit in 1998 payable to a husband and wife is about $20,000 a year. This amount may increase due to inflation.[3]	_____

[3]You can contact the Social Security Administration to determine your estimated retirement benefit by using form SSA-7004-SM-OP1. Most insurance professionals have these forms.

Step 3: Calculate the benefit you will receive from your employer's retirement plan at your retirement age. (1) If you are a participant in a defined benefit plan, you are entitled to a monthly benefit, which you can obtain from your plan administrator. (2) If you are a participant in a defined contribution plan such as profit sharing, 403(b), or 401(k), your retirement benefit is based on the sum total of your current account, future interest earned, future employer contributions, and future employee contributions. _____

Step 4: Calculate the amount of income, if any, you will receive from other sources. This includes personal savings or investments and the proceeds realized from the sale of a home or other property, including a business. _____

Step 5: Add the total amount of your anticipated income (Steps 2, 3, and 4). _____

Step 6: Subtract the number in Step 5 from Step 1. _____

Step 7: Calculate how much you need to save, if any, to make up the shortage shown in Step 6. This depends on the interest factor you assume, the number of years you have to save, and the amount of time you want your retirement benefit to last. (See case study below.) _____

CASE STUDY

Sam is a 50-year-old plant manager who wants to know if he is on track to meeting his retirement objectives. Sam currently earns $100,000 annually. He estimates his income will increase 4% each year until he retires. Using the retirement calculator, Sam's analysis shows:

Step 1: Annual retirement income objective (about 70% of future salary at age 65, which will be about $180,000): $126,000

Step 2: Assumed Social Security benefit:[4] $20,000

Step 3: Assumed retirement benefit from employer's pension and 401(k) plan:[5] $50,000

Step 4: Assumed income from personal investments:[6] $10,000

Step 5: Projected total income: (Steps 2+3+4) $80,000

[4]Sam is assuming Social Security benefits will not increase.
[5]To simplify matters, it is assumed that Sam's pension plan will provide him with a retirement benefit of 27% of his salary prior to retiring.
[6]Sam owns a bond fund which pays him about $10,000 annually.

Step 6:	Shortage: (Step 1 minus step 5)	$46,000
Step 7:	Amount of capital needed to generate $46,000 of income:[7]	$575,000
Step 8:	Annual savings needed to accumulate $575,000 in 15 years:[8]	$21,177

[7,8]Assuming 8% interest, Sam will need to save $21,177 for 15 years to accumulate $575,000 which can generate an annual income of $46,000 indefinitely. Less money is needed if Sam wants an income for only a specific period of time. For example, suppose he only wants to accumulate enough money to pay $46,000 per year for 15 years starting at age 65. At 8%, he would need about $451,635 instead of $575,000. Of course, if Sam lives more than 15 years, he would have no additional money.

LESSONS LEARNED

1. Decide which approach to retirement you should take, defined benefit or defined contribution.

2. Start saving as early as possible to benefit from compound growth.

3. Take into consideration other factors and sources of money when determining your retirement needs.

4. A disability caused by illness or injury can end your retirement program.

5. If you die before you retire, your family may have a minimal retirement benefit, or none at all.

CHAPTER 2

Financial Architecture: Creating a Portfolio Blueprint

PROFILE

Congratulations: You've begun a retirement plan! You are participating in your employer's plan or you are creating your own plan as a business owner. You are working on reaching one of the most important financial goals a person can set. Now you must make some decisions on what to do with the money you are accumulating!

For many people, the first question is: What product should I pick?

Actually, this is the *last* question in the retirement planning process. There are several steps involved in building a retirement portfolio. The pyramid in Figure 2-1 illustrates the steps, starting with the *most important* questions at the bottom.

When you build a portfolio for your retirement assets by thinking through these steps, you can control and monitor your portfolio more effectively. With this goal in mind, take the time to develop a "blueprint." Let's look at the pyramid in detail, starting with the first level.

LEVEL I: ESTABLISHING YOUR OBJECTIVES

The foundation of any portfolio starts with your time frame and financial goal. Outline for yourself the number of years to your

FIGURE 2-1

Financial Pyramid

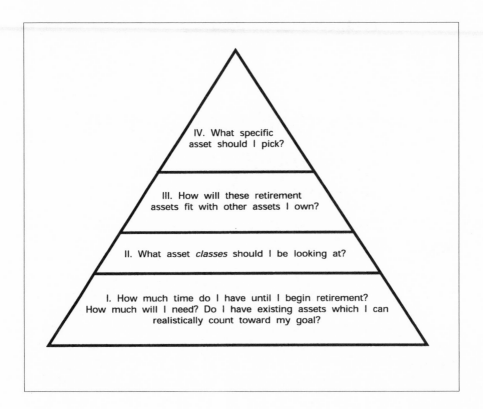

planned retirement date and the amount of money you hope to have accumulated at that time. As a general rule, the more time you have until you need the money, the more *market risk* you can afford to take. Consider other assets you plan to convert to retirement dollars, such as the proceeds from the sale of a home or business. The fewer dollars you need to accumulate, the less risk you must accept to reach your target.

Clarifying your timeline and final dollar objective gives overall shape to your portfolio decisions. You will know over time if you are on track. Because you have a plan, you will know if you need or want to make adjustments to your goals.

LEVEL II: ASSET CLASSES AND DIVERSIFICATION

The second level of the decision pyramid starts to color in details specific to you and your preferences by considering which *asset classes* are appropriate in your portfolio.

If we could build the "perfect product," we would probably want:

1. A product that never declined in value, and
2. Exceeded inflation, and
3. Produced a regular, fairly predictable income, and
4. Grew in value over time, and
5. Would be "hot" when the market is hot, and
6. Enjoyed favorable tax treatment.

Unfortunately, there is no single product that will do all this *all* the time. There isn't even a product that will deliver all these benefits *some* of the time! Add to this the fact that nobody knows what single product will perform best over the next 12 months and the process can look pretty overwhelming.

Fortunately, there is a method of moving forward with a sound and intelligent plan. Professionals recommend building a *diversified portfolio*, incorporating a mix of assets that perform differently in varying market conditions. While there is a multitude of different assets, most can be classified in one of four basic categories. These classes are listed below in order of least to most market risk, and least to most opportunity for principal growth:

1. Safety of Principal

The primary objective of this kind of asset is *minimum volatility* of the money committed to it. Such an asset is not expected to increase much in value, but it is not expected to decline either. These assets typically pay interest or dividends, which can create growth. Examples are money market accounts, whole life insurance policy cash values, certain annuities, and CDs.

There is little principal risk with these assets (in fact, some CDs are federally guaranteed to certain limits), but there is also little protection from inflation risk. In addition, because of the

impose an even lower ceiling. Susan will have to repay her loan within five years, unless it qualifies as an exception, for example, as a loan to buy a principal residence.

There is one important point that must be mentioned here. Very few plans permit a former employee to continue repaying a 401(k) plan loan. So if Susan leaves her job, she may have to repay the outstanding balance to avoid taxation. If she does not, the IRS will count it as an early distribution subject to income tax and possible penalty tax.

ESTATE PLANNING

The value of a 401(k) plan can be an important part of your estate. For example, let's suppose that as the years go by Susan has accumulated $150,000 in her account. She should make sure that she has designated a beneficiary for her account. It might be her spouse, children, or some other family member. The plan administrator provides participants with proper forms, but it is the particpant's responsibility to keep beneficiary designations current. Susan may not want her former spouse to get her money at her death.

Upon Susan's death, the account is usually paid quickly to her designated beneficiary. The distribution is generally reportable as income to the beneficiary. The 10% penalty tax for early withdrawals is waived at death. A surviving spouse has the option of rolling over the distribution to his or her own IRA (or other qualified plan, if allowed) and deferring the income tax. Due to this option, it is usually smart to name a spouse as primary beneficiary. If you want other individuals to receive a legacy at death, you can designate them as beneficiaries under your will or trust. For example, Susan may have accumulated investments— outside her 401(k)—which she may want to leave to her children. Susan could describe this property in her will and designate her children as the beneficiaries. Nonpension assets are typically not subject to income tax at death.

FUNDING OPTIONS

The money that Susan has contributed to her 401(k) can be allocated to one or more financial products being offered by her employer. The best asset allocation for Susan is the combination of investments that will give her the return she wants without too much risk. (See Chapter 2 for a discussion of investments and risk.) The three basic asset categories are cash, fixed income, and growth.

The funding options given to Susan in a 401(k) are preselected to offer her choices in each major asset class. Typically, 401(k) plans offer mutual funds or annuities which, on their own, have a basic level of diversification. When deciding how to allocate assets, Susan should consider all her assets, including those outside of her 401(k) plan. If she needs advice, she should select her own financial advisor. Her employer will not tell her which products to choose.

Susan's employer will keep Susan informed of how her investments are doing by sending her a financial statement of her 401(k) account at least once a year. Most plans will send either semiannually, quarterly, or on a monthly basis. This will show the amounts she has contributed and how well all of her investment accounts are performing.

LESSONS LEARNED

1. A 401(k) plan is a defined contribution plan because the contribution is known. The retirement income from a 401(k) depends on the future value of the account.

2. A 401(k) plan provides tax benefits. Contributions are made with pretax money; interest or growth is income tax-deferred; and lump sum distributions can be eligible for five-year averaging (until the year 2000).

3. An employee should contribute as much as possible to a 401(k) plan. To help employees save and to retain or recruit new employees, employers should match some of the employee's contributions.

4. 401(k) plans offer a participant a high level of flexibility and control over the plan. A participant decides how much to save (within limits) and how to invest (also within certain limits).

5. Keep beneficiary designations current.

6. An employer is legally responsible for the administrative supervision of the 401(k) plan it has sponsored. The employer must also make sure that participants have adequate information to make informed decisions about the plan.

7. When a participant leaves his or her current job, she will not lose the money that she has contributed nor the earnings on it. The participant must be sure to transfer the plan account into a new employer's 401(k) plan or to an IRA to defer income tax.

8. Although early withdrawals may not be the right way to go, borrowing from a 401(k) is a viable option, which has the advantage of qualifying the participant without a credit check.

9. If a participant leaves his current employment and has borrowed from his plan, the participant may have to repay the outstanding loan prior to a distribution being made or pay tax on the balance of the loan.

10. The benefits of starting to contribute to a 401(k) as soon as possible are the savings you will have accumulated when you retire, owing to compound growth.

5

Special (k): Adopting a 401(k) Plan to Meet Your Company's Needs

PROFILE

David and his spouse, Sheila, began Creative Designs Inc., an advertising and marketing business, 10 years ago. In the beginning it was really difficult convincing larger accounts that they could do the job. They did everything themselves, including artwork, marketing themes, layout, and seeing prospective clients to sell their services. Now, after struggling for some time, they are recognized as one of the most creative agencies in their area. As their business grew, so did their staff. They now employ over 20 people in various positions. Their accountant told them that in order to retain and attract high-quality employees, they should consider a retirement plan. When they spoke to their insurance agent, he recommended a 401(k) plan. During a meeting last week with their accountant and financial advisor, several options were offered. Now they have to make some decisions.

David and Sheila realized that the cost of adopting any plan other than a 401(k) would be too high. All other plans required comparable contributions for the employees compared to the contributions for David and Sheila. Since many of the employees were highly paid, that cost would be excessive.

401(K)

John explained that in a 401(k) plan, most of the contributions are made by the employees from their salaries before taxes are withheld. These contributions are called "employee deferrals." Since David and Sheila are also employees of the corporation, they too can make employee deferrals. John also explained that a 401(k) plan had to satisfy a nondiscrimination test to be sure that the plan was being used equitably by employees with high incomes and those with lower incomes.

This test, known as the "actual deferral percentage" (ADP) test, compares the contributions of the "highly compensated employees" to the "non-highly compensated employees." IRS regulations define highly compensated employees as any employee who earned $80,000 (for 1998) or more in the prior year or is a 5% or more owner. All other employees are considered non-highly compensated. As an incentive to participate, John suggested a small matching contribution based on the amount the employee defers. This would encourage more employees to participate and make it easier to pass the ADP test. John also pointed out that a 401(k) plan can require that employees be employed for at least one year, work 1000 hours during that year, and have reached their 21st birthday to be eligible to participate. David thought that those were good provisions to include in the plan.

After reviewing the list of employees, David determined that besides himself and Sheila, there were 15 other eligible employees. John suggested making a presentation to the employees to determine how much they would contribute so that he could determine how much David and Sheila could contribute. They decided that a match of 50% of the employee contribution, capped at 4% of salary, was affordable. This way, they knew that the maximum the company would have to contribute would be 2% of salary. John explained that most 401(k) plans allowed the employees to direct their own investments. By offering the option, the employees are more involved in the plan and are more likely to participate. John suggested one of the popular investment vehicles that allows the employees to make and change their investments through a toll-free telephone number. Each employee could choose from among several types of funds including growth, growth and income, corporate and government bond funds, international funds, and many others; there was something for everybody. In addition, the employees would receive quarterly statements showing all their contributions, including the matching contributions and the value of their account at the end of the quarter. Other options that John suggested were a loan provision and a hardship withdrawal. These options allow the employees to access their accounts under certain conditions, making them more likely to make deferrals, knowing they could take withdrawals in an emergency. After completing the survey, John summarized the results:

401(K) SUMMARY

	Salary	Deferral	Match	ADP%
David	$175,000	$10,000	$3,200	8.25
Sheila	175,000	10,000	3,200	8.25
Marketing director	85,000	4,000	1,700	6.71
			Average	7.74%
Artist A	75,000	3,000	1,500	6.00
Artist B	60,000	4,500	1,200	9.50
Layout A	55,000	0	0	0
Layout B	52,000	2,000	1,000	5.77
Marketing A	48,000	0	0	0
Marketing B	45,000	2,500	900	7.56
Marketing C	45,000	3,000	900	8.67
Receptionist	28,000	0	0	0
Secretary A	32,000	2,500	640	9.81
Secretary B	29,000	1,000	500	5.17
Secretary C	31,000	1,500	620	6.84
Office Manager	50,000	2,500	1,000	7.00
Bookkeeper	38,000	3,000	760	9.89
Driver	33,000	0	0	0
			Average	5.77%

Analyzing the results determined that the employees' average deferral was 5.77%. According to IRS guidelines, the highly compensated employees' average deferral percentage could be up to 7.77%. Since the marketing director's salary was over $80,000 last year, he too is a member of the highly compensated group. If David and Sheila each deferred $10,000 (the maximum for 1998), plus their match of $3,200, their percentage would be 8.25% ($13,200/$160,000—the maximum salary for 1998). Adding the percentage for the three highly compensated employees and dividing by three would give an average of 7.74%, within the maximum of 7.77%. The result of this would be a total before-tax contribution for David and Sheila of $26,400. The only contribution cost for the employees would be the matching contribution of $10,720, which was within David and Sheila's budget and was deductible from the company's taxable income.

To implement the plan, John was able to use a prototype plan document without charge from the insurance company that offered the investments to fund the benefits. The following week, John returned to meet with each employee and assist them in deciding how much to contribute and to which accounts to contribute, depending on their financial goals and risk profile.

LESSONS LEARNED

1. A 401(k) plan is funded mostly with employee deferrals, which are contributions made from employees' salaries.

2. The amount that can be contributed by the owners of a business depends on the amount contributed by the employees.

3. To encourage employee participation, a matching contribution should be included.

4. Other plan provisions that encourage employee participation are self-directed investments, loans, and hardship distribution provisions.

5. An experienced professional specializing in 401(k) plans should be consulted to assist in the design and installation of the plan.

6

Go with the Cash Flow:
Profit-Sharing Plans

PROFILE

When Jane graduated from law school and passed the bar, she went to work for a large downtown firm. Even though her salary was attractive, Jane did not like corporate politics and the lack of client contact. So at the age of 27, with the support of her family and with a little savings, she opened up her own law practice.

Jane's first strategy as a lawyer was to incorporate her practice as a professional corporation and lease an office from a small firm. For an additional fee she was able to use the firm's secretarial staff and library, the basic tools needed by any firm. Jane used her savings to pay several months of rent and to purchase furniture and a computer. The only things she really needed were clients.

Jane soon realized that the practice of law is not like "Field of Dreams." In the movie, Kevin Costner portrayed a farmer and baseball fan who built a baseball field in the middle of a cornfield so that the ghosts of famous baseball players would come to play ball. He knew that "if he built it, they would come." In law, Jane's clients were not coming. She needed paying clients if she was going to be able to pay her bills.

To gain clients, Jane created a business and marketing plan. She quickly discovered that the practice of law has many similarities to any other business. Jane's marketing plan emphasized using all of her contacts—friends, family, and lawyers she knew who had an overflow of cases, or those simply willing to help. She learned that for a business to succeed, you have to meet people, build confidence, get referrals, become known, and deliver a good and cost-effective product.

Jane's "product" was law. But she didn't have the luxury of practicing in areas where she had little or no experience. Thus, she began to specialize in the areas she was trained in by her past employer; real estate, estate planning, probate, and family law. These areas also made business sense to Jane because they generally involved transactions that are not tied up at length in court and they allowed extensive contact with clients. In other words, she could work fast and be paid quickly. To her surprise and benefit, she learned that almost everyone she met had an outdated estate plan. And soon, many of her clients were referring her to family members and friends who were getting remarried, divorced, adopting children, buying or selling a home, or trying to protect a parent's property for Medicaid purposes.

Jane's hard work and smart marketing started to pay off. In just three years of being in business, she now expects to earn over $170,000 in salary after expenses. Those expenses include a full-time assistant at a salary of $25,000 per year. As a profitable attorney and business owner, Jane wants to start saving for retirement. However, Jane has had very little experience with retirement planning and investments. To get help, she contacted her insurance professional, Sue.

Sue asked Jane questions in four key areas, eliciting the following responses:

1. *Retirement goals*: Due to her parents' comfortable retirement, Jane recognized the benefits and desired substantial savings for retirement.

2. *Ability to make future contributions to the retirement plan*: Despite her success, Jane was concerned about income over the next several years. She might need capital to hire an associate or move to a prestigious address.

3. *Desire for tax deductions*: Jane was very interested in income tax deductions for her business and understood

the value of compound interest accelerated by tax-deferred growth.

4. *Employee coverage by the plan*: Jane was very pleased with her employee, Sarah. Jane did not mind contributing toward Sarah's retirement if it could be done cost effectively and would encourage Sarah to stay with her.

Based on Jane's objectives, Sue advised her to create a qualified profit-sharing plan integrated with Social Security.

QUALIFIED PROFIT-SHARING PLAN—BENEFITS

A. PARTICIPATION AND VESTING

A qualified plan requires the employer to make contributions to all eligible employees and "vest" benefits pursuant to a specific schedule. Generally, eligibility means that all full-time employees over the age of 21 are eligible to participate. Employees, like Sarah, who work at least 1000 hours during the year, are considered full-time. Full-time employees under the age of 21 and part-time employees who work less than 1000 hours during the year may be excluded from participating in the plan.

B. PLAN CONTRIBUTIONS

A profit-sharing plan is a flexible plan in which the employer can make income tax-deductible contributions of 0% to 15% of participating payroll. This means Jane can tailor her contributions to meet her business needs. In years when cash is readily available, Jane can take advantage of the 15% maximum; in other years she can contribute less or nothing at all.

This is extremely important for most businesses. Whether the firm is a one-person shop like Jane's, or even a major law firm, the officers or partners of the business may not be sure of future income. They may want the flexibility to skip contributions if the money is not there or if it is needed for other business purposes.

C. ALLOCATING CONTRIBUTIONS

In a profit-sharing plan, "annual additions" cannot exceed the lesser of 25% of salary or $30,000. Annual additions include employer contributions, employee contributions, and forfeitures. This is not to be confused with the 15% limitation on employer deductible contributions. The allocation limitation should not adversely affect young business owners for two reasons. First, the maximum contribution limit is high. Second, young business owners and professionals like Jane have many years until they retire. They can enjoy decades of contributions made on their behalf, which grow tax-deferred. For example, if Jane's firm was only able to contribute to her account $20,000 annually for 30 years and it earned a hypothetical rate of 8% each year, she would have $2,265,664 at retirement. That's why it pays to contribute as much as possible and start as soon as you can.

One method of allocating plan contributions is proportionate to pay. For example, if a participant's pay is 10% of eligibile payroll, she or he gets 10% of the contribution. However, a qualified plan may be "integrated" with Social Security. A plan integrated with Social Security skews the contribution in favor of more highly compensated employees. Integrating the profit-sharing plan means, in effect, that Jane gets credit for contributions to Social Security that she was already making for her employee, thus it reduces her obligation to make contributions for that employee in her private plans. Table 6-1 shows the allocation between an integrated plan and a nonintegrated plan.

TABLE 6-1

Integration vs. Nonintegration

	Compensation	Integrated Allocation*	Nonintegrated
Jane	$160,000 (1998 max.)	$24,705	$24,000
Sarah	25,000	3,045	3,750
		$27,750	$27,750

*Based upon 1998 Social Security wage base.

The difference between the two plans is that the integrated formula provides Jane with $705 more contributions each year, and her outlay to the employee (Sarah) is reduced.

Even though Jane is contributing on behalf of Sarah, the profit-sharing plan is still cost effective. The income tax savings generated more than offset the contribution Jane has to make for her employee.

The cost of providing a benefit to an employee can also be offset in nonfinancial ways. First, a valuable benefit is provided to the employee. Second, a generous retirement plan can help retain and attract employees. (See Table 6-2).

D. VESTING

A vesting schedule provides that after a specified number of years, allocated money to an employee's account cannot be forfeited or lost if employment is terminated, regardless of the reason. For example, suppose after a number of years, Sarah's retirement account is worth $50,000 and she is fully vested. If Sarah walks into Jane's office, quits without notice, and even takes some of Jane's clients, she is entitled to the full value of her account. She gets the money pursuant to the terms established in the plan.

Jane's plan is considered "top heavy," which means that plan assets allocated to "key employees" exceed 60% of all plan assets. In general, a key employee is an owner of the business or officer. When a plan is top heavy, there typically is a choice of two vesting schedules. The first schedule permits an employer to design the plan so that no employee is vested until he or she completes three years of service. Then the employee is 100% vested. The second schedule is graded over time. The employee is vested in 20% of his or her account after two years of service, then 20% more each year until after six years, he or she is 100% vested.

If a business owner thinks employees will leave after three to five years of service, a graded schedule is better. A terminating employee would forfeit nonvested benefits, which are then allocated to the other participants.

TABLE 6-2

Plan Analysis

Employer contribution	$27,750
Income tax savings (assumed 35% tax rate)	9,713
After-tax cost of plan	18,037
Jane's allocation	24,705
Net gain	6,668*

*In this example gain refers to the portion of the income savings that accrue to Jane's account. This savings does not take into consideration income tax due on distributions.

E. OTHER BENEFITS

As a qualified retirement plan, a profit-sharing plan has important tax and legal benefits. For example, contributions are income tax-deductible and not reportable as income to the employee
participant. In addition, interest or growth on the investments in
the plan is income tax-deferred until it is withdrawn. This is important for someone like Jane, who is starting to earn a high income from her business.

Profit-sharing money is exempt from claims of employer creditors. Once the employer makes the contribution, it is segregated
from the employer's assets. This means that if the employer goes
bankrupt, its creditors cannot attach any of the plan's assets.

Profit-sharing money is also exempt from most claims of the
employee's creditors. In general, a creditor cannot attach assets
inside of a qualified plan belonging to an employee. However, if
an employee owes money to the IRS or to a former spouse pursuant to a dissolution of marriage, or owes money to a child for
support, then qualified plan money may be attachable under a
"qualified domestic relations order" (QDRO).

Creditor protection can be important to any business owner
or plan participant. While most people are probably not overly
concerned with creditor protection laws, our society is quite liti-
gious. Protecting assets is simply a smart strategy to utilize when
it is available.

F. GETTING STARTED

A profit-sharing plan is easy for a business owner to create. The
first step is to draft a plan document. There are generally two ways

of doing this. The first way is to contact an attorney or a retirement plan specialist who will custom design a plan document based on the specific needs of the employer. The second way is to adopt a plan document that has been preapproved by the IRS. These plans are commonly referred to as "prototypes." The insurance company that Sue represents offers its policyholders a preapproved profit-sharing plan that can be adopted by an employer. A good prototype document is usually sufficient for most business owners.

In order for an employer to make tax-deductible contributions, the plan must be in force prior to the end of the business tax year. Jane's firm is on a calendar year, so the prototype plan must be adopted before December 31st. However, the law permits contributions to be made at any time up until the due date of the employer's tax return, including extensions. This gives employers like Jane time to analyze her business affairs to determine how much can be contributed.

Jane should realize that waiting until the last minute to make a contribution is not always the best choice. The reason is that the sooner the contribution is made, the faster tax-deferred interest can be earned on the money.

Once the plan is in force, each employee should receive a summary plan description. This is a summary of all the major benefits of the plan. For example, it lets the employees know the name of the trustee and procedures to follow in the event of a claim. In addition, each employee should receive a statement regarding the value of his or her account, which will show the amount of the contribution allocated to the account and all interest or growth earned during the prior year.

Finally, the employer is required to file IRS Form 5500. A third-party pension administrator or the company's accountant usually files this form. No employer should forget to file. The IRS can charge substantial penalties for not filing.

LESSONS LEARNED

1.   A profit-sharing plan can offer many tax and financial benefits to an employer. Contributions are income tax-deductible and interest is tax-deferred.

2.   A profit-sharing plan allows flexible contributions. Thus, it is an ideal plan to use where income or profits may not be steady over a given number of years.

3.   A traditional profit-sharing plan is an ideal type of retirement plan for younger employees or younger business owners. This is because there is a substantial amount of time until retirement, allowing employees to enjoy many years of both deductible contributions and tax-deferred growth of money.

4.   Profit-sharing plans can be easy to create and relatively simple to administer. However, there are specific rules that must be followed.

5.   Profit sharing plan documents can be custom designed by an attorney or can be pre-approved by the IRS and adopted as a prototype plan.

CHAPTER 7

Two for Your Money: Combining Defined Contribution Plans

PROFILE

John is a 32-year-old owner of a business that provides decorative signs for storefronts. After several years, John has gone from "hustling" his work and occasional contracts to ongoing referrals and success. With positive cash flow came the hiring of an employee and the luxury of planning for the future and eventual retirement. John also incorporated his business and is now known as Signing Star Inc.

John is married and has two young children. His wife works part-time, helps John with the business, and takes care of their children.

To begin his quest for an enriched retirement, John met with his insurance professional, David, to discuss qualified retirement plans. In response to David's questions regarding his plan goals, John explained:

1. *Contributions*: He wants to save or contribute as much as possible. John has middle-aged friends who are now scrambling to save sufficient dollars for retirement.

2. *Income tax deductions*: He wants to reduce his income tax as much as possible.

sion consultant suggested a defined benefit plan, since a defined contribution plan is limited to a $30,000 annual contribution.

There was no money left in the corporation to fund the plan, and John couldn't reduce his salary without reducing the pension contribution below $50,000. John needed a unique funding approach. The consulting firm suggested that John loan the corporation $50,000 to fund the plan. Since the pension deduction would create a $50,000 loss to the corporation, that loss would pass through to John's personal tax return (on form K-1) and would save him $22,500 in taxes (in a 45% federal and state income tax bracket). If John withdrew $27,500 from his savings, he could fund the plan with the savings plus the money he would have paid in taxes. By transferring the money from taxable savings to the corporation so it can fund the pension plan, the earnings on the $27,500 would also be deferred from income taxes.

Indirectly, John is sheltering his personal income, salary, interest, dividends, etc., through the use of a corporate pension deduction.

CASE STUDY #5

GOOD FOR THE EMPLOYEES, BETTER FOR THE OWNERS

Harvey Woods founded Woods Electronics Inc., with his brother Jack 10 years ago. After three years of struggling, he took in two "partners" to improve the company's cash position so they could compete with extended research and development. Each partner now owns 20 percent of Woods Electronics Inc., and Harvey and Jack each own 30 percent. The company's specialty is research funded by government contracts, which are extremely erratic. Political pressure can cause funding to stop or decrease with little notice. Despite this, the company is finally in a position to fund a retirement plan but wants the plan to favor the owners and long-term employees and be flexible enough to match their business cycles.

Harvey's insurance agent suggested a unique profit-sharing plan based on a change in the law that was part of the Tax Reform Act of 1986. This plan defines separate groups of employees, usually based on their job descriptions, and defines a specific contribution for each group. The value of each employee's annual contributions and investment earnings on the contributions are then projected to retirement age and converted to an annuity benefit, i.e., monthly retirement benefits. These benefits must not discriminate in favor of highly compensated employees, an employee whose salary is more than $80,000 (in the prior year) or who is a 5% or more owner.

The advantage of this type of plan is the ability to allocate the majority of the contribution to owners and key employees, as compared to the typical profit-sharing plan. The disadvantage is the higher cost of establishing the plan and the annual administration. In general, the savings realized on the reduction of employees' contributions more than compensate for any additional maintenance costs. The result of the plan designed for Woods Electronics Inc. is illustrated and compared to a traditional profit-sharing plan in Table 12-5.

As you can see, the results are favorable. The owers have maintained their contribution level but reduced the total plan contribution by $65,660. This is the difference between the traditional profit-sharing contribution of $175,482 and the nontraditional profit-sharing contribution of $109,822. These savings can be used to help fund a nonqualified retirement program for selected key employees and/or the owners and enhance their retirement benefits even further.

You may also wonder why the contribution for the owners is only $20,500 each ($82,000 ÷ 4) rather than $30,000, the annual contribution limit. Profit-sharing and 401(k) plans are both types of defined contribution plans. As such, the maximum allocation to an employee in both plans cannot exceed $30,000. The balance of the partners' contribution is funded through their 401(k) plan, another efficient vehicle for leveraging contributions (see Chapters 4 and 5).

TABLE 12-5

CONTRIBUTION ALLOCATION	
Job Class	Total Contribution (% of salary)
Owners and officers	12.81%
Engineers	3%
Other employees	3%

COMPARISON OF TRADITIONAL AND NONTRADITIONAL PROFIT-SHARING PLANS*					
Job Class	No. in Class	Traditional Profit-Sharing Plan	Percentage of Total Contribution	Woods Nontraditional Profit Plan Contribution	Percentage of Total Contribution
Owners and officers	4	$82,000	46.73%	$82,000 ·	74.66%
Engineers	5	$46,588	26.55%	$12,923	11.77%
Other employees	16	$46,894	26.72%	$14,899	13.57%
Total	25	$175,482	100.00%	$109,822	100.00%

*Effective date of Woods Electronics Inc., profit-sharing plan January 1, 1999.

LESSONS LEARNED

1. Professional firms and corporations that have key employees (usually owners or partners) can increase retirement benefits by creating retirement plans for different classes of employees.

2. Defined benefit plans can be based on prior year's salary.

3. Selling the assets of your company but keeping your corporation can help you maintain an attractive retirement plan and offset the gain on the sale.

4. Loaning money to your corporation can help the company fund your retirement plan on a tax-deductible basis and offset other personal income.

5. Separate classification of employees can reduce retirement contributions for non-highly compensated employees.

6. Nontraditional retirement plans can be used to accomplish financial goals other than retirement.

CHAPTER 13

Give and Ye Shall Receive: The Benefits of Rewarding Key Employees

PROFILE

Gordon Davis is one of the most trusted and valued employees of J&M Electronics, a 20-year-old family business owned by two brothers, Jack and Marty. The company employs more than 50 people and has four locations. In addition, there are two more stores on the drawing board.

Despite their achievements to date, the success of J&M's expansion from four stores to six may greatly depend on how hard Gordon Davis is willing to work in the future. Gordon has worked for J&M for more than 10 years and knows every aspect of the retail electronics business. Currently, he operates J&M's most successful store, earns $125,000 per year, and is J&M's most highly paid employee (excluding Jack and Marty, who earn more).

If Gordon is willing to stay on and work hard during this difficult growth period, Jack and Marty have promised him "significant financial rewards down the road if the new stores are successful," but probably not major stock ownership. Both Jack and Marty have agreed that control of the company will remain in the hands of their family.

Gordon is 50 years old and will be at least 53 by the time the new stores open. Due to the high cost of financing their expansion, Jack and Marty cannot afford to pay Gordon more salary today. In addition, it is now critical for them to keep their corporate balance sheet strong so they can borrow when necessary to help finance their expansion. Gordon knows all of this and has expressed concern about his retirement planning, overall financial security, and his future employment.

Gordon has a wife and two children who depend on him. He has little retirement savings, and the small contribution made by J&M to its SEP-IRA each year (for all its employees) is not enough to secure even a modest retirement for him. These issues must be addressed in order to convince Gordon to stay and help make the expansion a success.

To complicate matters, a large Sears recently opened for business in the next town. Not only are they looking to hire an experienced general manager but they also have asked Gordon to interview for the job.

Solution

Jack and Marty have agreed that if they don't do something special for Gordon today, they will lose him. Of all the strategies used by employers to provide unique benefits to their employees, Jack and Marty have agreed on providing Gordon and his family with a program of true deferred compensation. The program would provide certain predefined retirement benefits for Gordon at age 65 and predefined survivorship death benefits for Gordon's spouse and children if he dies before his retirement benefits are fully paid. See the box below and Figure 13-1 for the precise schedule of benefits.

KEY BENEFITS OF GORDON'S DEFERRED COMPENSATION PROGRAM

1. If Gordon stays with J&M for 15 years and reaches normal retirement age, he will receive from J&M a retirement benefit of $50,000 per year for the next 15 years, i.e., until age 80, totaling $750,000.

2. If Gordon dies before age 65, his family will immediately receive the same $50,000 per year as a death benefit for the next 15 years, totaling $750,000.

3. If Gordon reaches normal retirement age but dies during the 15-year retirement period, his spouse and family will continue to receive the balance of the 15-year income as a death benefit.

FIGURE 13-1

Life Insurance Company

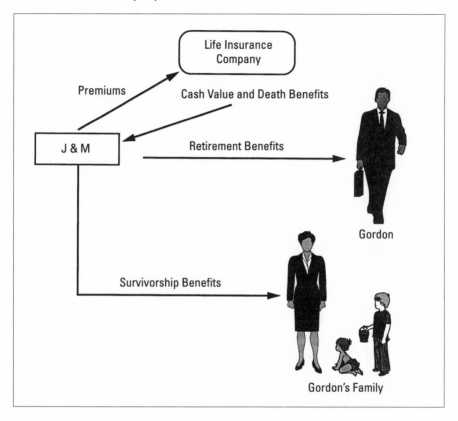

Funding with Life Insurance

Based on this benefit schedule, J&M will contractually agree to pay deferred compensation benefits to Gordon when he retires at age 65 or to his family at his death. The benefits can be informally funded with life insurance on Gordon's life. (As we shall see later, life insurance can be an effective way to help pay benefits.) The corporation will be the owner and beneficiary of the policy. The cash values of the insurance can grow tax-deferred and be used to help pay the retirement benefits portion of the deferred compensation. In addition, the death proceeds of the insurance can be used to help pay the death benefits portion of the deferred compensation.

J&M will pay annual premiums—without any out-of-pocket

cost to Gordon. In essence, J&M will be providing Gordon and his family with $750,000 of benefits ($50,000 each year for 15 years at retirement or death). When retirement or death benefits are paid, they will be income taxable to the recipient (Gordon or his family).

The cash value of the insurance will appear on the books of the corporation as an asset, and until benefits are paid, it will be fully subject to the claims of J&M's general creditors. To maximize this corporate benefit, J&M will select a life insurance policy that has large early cash value growth. This can help keep the company's balance sheet looking strong and reduce any annual charges to corporate earnings that may result from paying non-deductible insurance premiums.

Under the program, Gordon will be 50% vested in all benefits after five years and 100% vested after 10 years. But even though Gordon is vested, he cannot have access to his retirement account until he retires or terminates employment. Gordon's benefits are not taxed until received because they are subject to the claims of J&M's corporate creditors.

The vesting schedule can be changed if the parties subsequently agree. In fact, deferred compensation is flexible enough so that any of its provisions can be changed if both parties agree. Generally, it's important to include a vesting schedule in deferred compensation programs because that way, if the employee leaves employment before age 65, he will be guaranteed some retirement and death benefits. Voluntary contributions to deferred compensation programs are usually 100% vested. (Note: The vesting schedule described here should not be confused with vesting in qualified pension or profit-sharing plans.)

One primary reason for an employer like J&M to use life insurance as an informal funding vehicle is to avoid using working capital to pay benefits. The promised benefit can be paid from cash values (if sufficient) or from the death proceeds of the policy.

Jack and Marty realize that deferred compensation benefits paid by J&M to Gordon and his family are income-tax–deductible to the corporation. They further realize that the cost to the corporation of providing these benefits is reduced by the economic value of the income-tax deduction received by the corporation. As the corporation's tax bracket increases, the after-tax cost of paying deductible benefits decreases. For example, if J&M pays Gordon $50,000 as deferred salary and the corporation is in a hypothetical 35% tax bracket, the annual cost to the eomployer is $32,500 ($50,000 – 35%, or $17,500). This is advantageous to companies like J&M, whose profits are expected to increase due to expansion. Finally, they realize that the after-tax cost to the corporation of providing benefits and paying premiums can be recouped from the death proceeds paid to the corporation at Gordon's death if the corporation keeps the insurance policy in force even after all benefits are paid. Depending on the amount of death proceeds paid at death, and when death occurs, the corporation may even be able to recoup its after-tax cost plus an interest factor to compensate it for the cost of the use of its money.

When Jack and Marty informed Gordon of the special retirement program they were going to provide only him if he stayed, Gordon canceled his interview with Sears.

DEFERRED COMPENSATION IMPLEMENTATION REQUIREMENTS

1. A resolution of the board of directors adopting the deferred compensation arrangement.

2. An agreement written by an attorney that sets forth the terms of the arrangement.

3. Written notification to the Department of Labor stating that a deferred compensation program is being implemented.

THE NEED FOR ADDITIONAL COMPENSATION

Most successful businesses make some type of contribution to a pension, profit-sharing, 401(k), or individual retirement account on behalf of rank-and-file employees. These contributions, however, may not be sufficient to satisfy the company's highly compensated employees, such as top salespeople and executives. In order to dissuade these valuable employees from seeking employment opportunities elsewhere (possibly with competitors who provide better benefits, as seen in our case study), the employer must somehow arrange to provide these employees with increased retirement benefits to keep them happy. At the same time, the employer may even provide similar or better benefits for himself or herself.

For most companies, it's nearly impossible to unilaterally increase qualified plan retirement benefits for highly compensated employees. To do so, the employer usually would have to increase benefits for all employees. That's because under the terms of the Employee Retirement Income Security Act (ERISA) (sometimes referred to as "Every Rotten Idea Since Adam"), qualified plans cannot discriminate in favor of highly compensated employees. Also, Congress continues to reduce the maximum amount of compensation that can be used to calculate qualified plan contributions and benefits for highly compensated employees. Before the Revenue Reconciliation Act of 1993, a qualified retirement plan could not base contributions or benefits on compensation above $235,840. The 1993 Act reduced this cap to $150,000, indexed for inflation. This amount has increased in 1998 to $160,000 and may go up slowly in future years. The salary cap is the maximum salary on which contributions can be based. As a direct result of this reduction, nonqualified deferred compensation arrangements have become increasingly popular, not just for key employees but for business owners who are also employees!

DEFERRED COMPENSATION OPTIONS IN DESIGN

Generally, the term *deferred compensation* is defined as a nonqualified retirement program created by an employer for select key executives and upper management. In sharp contrast to qualified pension and profit-sharing plans, which require almost all employees to be eligible to participate, nonqualified deferred compensation arrangements offer an employer the opportunity to discriminate as to overall participation in the program.

Deferred compensation arrangements are typically designed to provide supplemental income to the executive at retirement and/or death benefits to the family should the executive die before retirement. The retirement income is usually paid in monthly installments for a given period of time. The deferred compensation death benefit is usually paid over time, but can be paid in one lump sum.

TYPES OF DEFERRED COMPENSATION

There are actually two types of deferred compensation: (1) a true deferred compensation program and (2) a supplemental executive retirement program (SERP). In a true deferred compensation program, the executive agrees to defer an upcoming raise or bonus or reduce future salary to pay for program benefits. On the other hand, with a SERP the executive is offered these benefits as a perquisite in addition to all other compensation. A SERP is what J&M Electronics offered Gordon Davis. The arrangement can also be a hybrid of the two programs, where the employer pays for some benefits, as in a SERP, and the executive pays for the rest, as in true deferred compensation. Sometimes deferred compensation is referred to as a salary continuation, "top hat," "golden handcuff," "401(k) lookalike," or "401(k) carve-out program."

CONTRACTUAL OBLIGATIONS AND FUNDING

Typically, the employer and executive enter into a written agreement in which the employer promises to provide certain retirement benefits to the executive and/or death benefits to family members at the executive's death. As previously stated, contributions may consist of employer contributions, executive deferrals, or a combination of both.

Promised benefits can be subject to forfeiture by the employee for reasons such as early termination of employment (usually prior to a specified date). This usually would not apply in a true deferred compensation scenario where benefits are paid with the employee's own money.

Deferred compensation programs should be (and are considered) "unfunded" or "informally" funded. This means that money or products used to pay benefits are not set apart from the employer's general assets and are reachable by the employer's creditors. For the employer, this is necessary to avoid the burdens of qualified plan reporting, funding, and ERISA discrimination regulations. For the executive, this is necessary to avoid current income taxation on contributions held by the employer to pay future benefits.

Deferred compensation benefit formulas can usually be designed in one of two ways. The first way is a defined contribution or money purchase formula. That is, the amount of money going in is known, but the future benefit is undetermined, for example, an annual deposit of 10% of salary or a fixed contribution, e.g., $10,000. The ultimate benefit payable will depend upon the interest earned or growth rate of the products purchased and the number of years in which contributions are made. In contrast, an employer can promise a benefit under a defined benefit formula. For example, the benefit could be 10% of final salary or a fixed benefit, e.g., $10,000 a year for a given number of years. The annual amount going into the plan is unknown but can be determined by using interest and growth rate assumptions. (This is the type of program offered to Gordon in our opening profile.)

Financial products purchased to help pay deferred compensation benefits are purchased and owned by the employer and appear on the corporate balance sheet as assets. When the executive dies or retires, benefits can be paid in one lump sum or over a specified period of time. The method of paying benefits should be spelled out in the deferred compensation agreement. The executive (or his/her beneficiary) will pay income tax on benefits when they are received. At that time, the employer will obtain an income tax deduction, as long as the amount paid is considered reasonable compensation.

BENEFITS OF DEFERRED COMPENSATION TO THE EMPLOYER

A deferred compensation arrangement provides many benefits to the employer:

- It helps the employer attract and retain key personnel.
- It permits the employer to handpick the employees who will participate in the program.
- Deferred compensation benefits are flexible.
- Deferred compensation benefits need not be immediately vested.
- The arrangement can be discontinued by the employer at any time (if provided in the contract).
- The arrangement requires no government approval.
- The arrangement requires no ongoing ERISA reporting.

- If structured correctly, informal funding of the arrangement by the employer can have little or no ultimate charge to earnings.
- Deferred compensation benefits are deductible by the corporation when paid, if they are reasonable.
- Deferred compensation benefits can be provided to selected top employees in addition to qualified pension and/or profit-sharing plan benefits.

BENEFITS OF DEFERRED COMPENSATION TO THE EXECUTIVE

Deferred compensation arrangements provide many benefits to the executive as well:

- They provide a supplemental retirement income for the executive.
- They provide a preretirement death benefit for the executive's family.
- The executive's current income can be deferred on a pretax basis.
- Benefits can be increased to help keep pace with inflation and future salary increases.
- Benefits are not taxable until received—except for FICA tax on contributions that produce vested benefits.
- Benefits can be designed to suit the specific needs of each executive.
- Benefits may eliminate or reduce the need for the executive to own large amounts of personal life insurance.
- Benefits may eliminate or reduce the need for the executive to invest personal after-tax dollars in supplemental retirement plans.
- Benefits can offset the reverse discrimination that may occur due to the Social Security integration of qualified retirement plan benefits.
- Death proceeds can be arranged to be free of federal estate tax [death benefit only (DBO) plan].

TAX CONSIDERATIONS OF DEFERRED COMPENSATION

During Employment

As long as the executive remains an unsecured creditor of the corporation in her or his deferred compensation benefit (which means that accumulated contributions and benefits are not made available to nor are they accessible by the executive), there is no immediate income taxation to the executive, even if the executive is fully vested. However, deferrals will be subject to FICA tax if the executive is vested. Recognition of income by the executive occurs upon either of the following:

1. *Constructive receipt*: When the executive has the ability to access benefits without leaving employment.
2. *Economic or financial benefit is conferred*: When the executive has actually received something of economic value.

Typically, the corporation is the owner of any assets used to "informally" fund the arrangement. Current outlays by the corporation to informally fund deferred compensation benefits are not currently tax deductible.

At the Executive's Retirement

At retirement, the executive begins receiving from the employer an annual, quarterly, or monthly deferred compensation retirement benefit. As benefits are paid, there is no longer a "substantial risk of forfeiture" with respect to them, and the executive is in actual receipt of them. At that time, the executive pays income tax on the amounts received. In addition, Social Security (FICA) taxes are due on all deferrals when they are vested which could be earlier than at payout.

It is important to note that the rights of a person to deferred compensation are subject to a "substantial risk of forfeiture" if they are subject to the claims of corporate creditors. When an employee terminates employment and is entitled to receive benefits, the lack of a substantial risk of forfeiture triggers the taxation of benefits as they are received. As long as the employer's obligation under the deferred compensation arrangement is merely an unfunded (or informally funded) and unsecured promise to pay, unpaid amounts will not be taxed to the executive.

At the Executive's Death

When the executive dies (either before or after retirement), the executive's beneficiary starts receiving from the employer an annual, quarterly, or monthly deferred compensation death benefit. Death benefits paid by the employer are taxable income to the executive's beneficiary when they are received. However, the amount of estate tax paid by the executive's estate on this amount, if any, is deductible (as a miscellaneous itemized deduction—not subject to the 2% floor) by the beneficiary against this income. The employer receives an income-tax deduction for each deferred compensation payment made because the payments are considered deferred salary. In most situations, the discounted or present value of the deferred compensation death benefit is included in the executive's gross estate for federal estate tax purposes. Benefits paid to a surviving spouse, however, should qualify for the estate tax unlimited marital deduction and therefore be estate tax-free.

PROTECTING BENEFITS FROM MANAGEMENT: RABBI TRUSTS

A conflict in designing deferred compensation arrangements occurs when the employee wishes to protect his or her rights in amounts deferred while at the same time avoiding current income taxation. A rabbi trust may provide some security for the employee. The term "rabbi trust" came about because the first person to avail himself of this technique was, in fact, a Rabbi whose congregation was providing him with deferred compensation.

In a rabbi trust arrangement, the employer contributes a certain amount to a trust each year while the employee is performing services for the employer. The employer will accumulate enough funds in the trust to cover the payments that will have to be made when the employee retires, thus avoiding a cash crunch for the employer. Under this arrangement, the funds placed in the trust still remain subject to the claims of corporate creditors, and the trust is therefore considered unfunded. Thus, if the employer is forced into bankruptcy, the employee may not receive anything. The good news, however, is that the accrued benefits are subject to a "substantial risk of forfeiture" and will remain untaxed to the executive. A benefit of a rabbi trust is that retirement funds or financial products purchased to help pay benefits are separated from management. The trust may own life insurance, mutual funds, bonds, or other products, which are earmarked only for paying benefits. Management may have no right to those products other than to pay benefits.

Typically, a rabbi trust specifies (1) when amounts will be paid to the executive and (2) the conditions the executive must satisfy (or which must occur) in order for payments to commence. These conditions are often called "triggering events." An important issue is whether the mere existence of a particular "trigger" in a deferred compensation arrangement will cause the executive to be deemed in constructive receipt of the deferred amounts, and therefore taxed on them, even though the amounts are not actually received. In various cases and rulings, the IRS has determined that the existence of one or more of the following triggering events does not put the executive in constructive receipt of funds held by the employer and thus effectively can be used to determine when deferred compensation benefits should commence:

- The executive becomes totally disabled.
- The executive attains a certain age.
- The executive's employment is terminated.
- The executive becomes a part-time employee.
- The executive becomes a director, partner, or officer of a competitor.

PROTECTING BENEFITS FROM CORPORATE CREDITORS: SECULAR TRUSTS

Secular trusts provide an ironclad guarantee that all deferred compensation funds will be there when the executive retires. But that comes at a price: The funds held by the employer to pay future benefits are currently income taxable to the employee. This may not be so bad for business owners with marginal personal income tax brackets of 28% if their marginal corporate income tax rate is 34%. Furthermore, because money contributed to a secular trust is taxable each year to the employee, it is deductible by the employer. Typically, the employer gives the employee a bonus at the end of each year to help pay this income tax.

Despite the potential tax savings available due to the differential in personal versus corporate brackets, the main benefit of using a secular trust is to provide protection and security against a potential corporate bankruptcy.

DEFERRED COMPENSATION FUNDING CONSIDERATIONS

Many employers who sponsor deferred compensation arrangements realize the importance of providing for their future obligations under the arrangements by making regular contributions so that the funds will be available when needed. Ways of funding deferred compensation obligations include:

1. Pay as you go
2. Sinking fund
3. Cash value life insurance

Pay as You Go

The pay-as-you-go approach means that the employer utilizes working capital or draws on its line of credit to make benefit payments as they become due. The advantage of this method is that it postpones the impact on working capital until a later date. The only immediate requirement of this approach is that a bookkeeping entry be made to accrue a deferred compensation liability on the corporate balance sheet. When benefits are payable, however, management must face the actual cash requirements of the deferred compensation program. At that time, the business may be faced with the need to generate sufficient operating capital to pay benefits in addition to normal operating expenses.

Sinking Fund

In a deferred compensation program, employer contributions and executive deferrals are leveraged by putting them at risk in the employer's business. Therefore, the promised benefit is only as secure as the employer promising it. A prudent decision would be to set aside assets in anticipation of future obligations. In order to do this, one must determine which asset(s) to use and just how much should be set aside. Although an endless array of funding vehicles are available to the employer, the choices are usually more limited when considering the importance of liquidity as well as risk versus reward. Long-term assets with a reasonable rate of return are generally preferred for deferred compensation programs.

Mutual funds (including stock and bond funds), for example, may be an attractive alternative, but the annual interest or income and capital gains of these funds may be subject to corporate income tax. Note: seventy percent of dividends may be eligible for the tax exclusion to a C corporation. Also, should the employee die before retirement, these and similar investments may not have had enough time to generate the needed cash to cover the employer's benefit obligation.

Cash Value Life Insurance

Cash value life insurance can be an ideal product to help accumulate money to pay benefits. Its benefits include:

- Insurance cash value growth is tax-deferred.
- Over time, insurance cash value growth may compare favorably with other financial products and may be used to help the employer pay retirement benefits.
- Death proceeds are paid income tax-free. Life insurance death proceeds may be subject to the alternative minimum tax (AMT) if the beneficiary of the policy is a C corporation. However, this tax is credited against future corporate taxes payable, with an unlimited carry forward. Corporations with less than $7,500,000 of receivables are not subject to AMT.
- Cash value can be borrowed or surrendered on a tax-favored basis if the policy is not classified as a modified endowment contract. (Borrowing or surrendering policy values will reduce the death benefit, and loans require interest to be paid.)

15

Double Your Advantage: Use Your Retirement Plan to Help Protect Your Estate

PROFILE

Bob Goodie is 100% shareholder, president, and CEO of a successful computer software development company located in Charlotte, North Carolina. Bob established the company, Goodie Disks, Inc., just five years ago. Now it employs 15 people on a full-time basis, including Bob's daughter, Rachel, who works there as a computer programmer. Bob is 52 years old and his wife, Helen, is 50. Helen works in the business as a part-time bookkeeper.

Bob and Helen have been happily married for 30 years. They have two children, Rachel and Aaron. Rachel is married and also has two children. Her husband, Tony, is a high school science teacher. Aaron is single and lives in Nashville. He is a struggling studio musician and has no interest in the computer software business.

Bob Goodie has never bothered to value his company, but last year, a buyer offered him $1,500,000 for it, as long as he would agree to stay on and work for the buyer as his employee. After being laid off from a good job once, Bob promised himself that he would never again work for anyone else, so he refused the offer. But the amount of the offer amazed him. He never thought his little software company would ever be worth so much. What if it turned out to be worth even more? This started Bob thinking about his net worth, his financial responsibility to his family, and his estate planning.

Before Bob went into business, he worked for IBM in software development. He was recruited directly from graduate school and worked there for 25 years, until he was unexpectedly let go in 1991. Bob was surprised to learn that he had accumulated over $500,000 in his tax-qualified profit-sharing plan account. When he left, Bob rolled over this amount into a personal IRA. When he established his own company, Bob "rolled back" this money into his own corporate profit-sharing plan, and owing to the incredible appreciation in the stock market in the last five years, this amount has tripled in value to $1,500,000.

Bob and Helen were shocked when they looked at their net worth for federal estate tax purposes. In addition to their $1,500,000 business and $1,500,000 profit-sharing plan, they had a $500,000 investment portfolio and a $500,000 personal residence. Their net worth was in excess of $4,000,000. That was the good news. The bad news was that at the death of the surviving spouse, they estimated that the combined federal estate taxes and federal income taxes on this amount could total $1,608,000. Where would this money come from?

It became crystal clear to Bob and Helen that without proper planning either their business or their profit-sharing plan would have to be liquidated to pay taxes. This would either prevent Rachel from inheriting a successful business or prevent Aaron, Rachel, and their grandchildren from inheriting their profit-sharing plan. Both options were unacceptable.

In addition to their estate tax problem, Bob and Helen became increasingly concerned about what might happen to their grandchildren if Rachel or Tony (or both) died unexpectedly. Who would take care of them? How would they afford college? Like most young couples, Rachel and Tony needed both of their incomes to live. If one of them died, the other would have a very difficult time supporting their children.

The question is: Can Bob and Helen take advantage of this opportunity by purchasing insurance in their profit-sharing plan? The answer is *yes*! Typically, if a business owner's estate is illiquid and there is a need for life insurance to help pay estate taxes, using profit-sharing assets to buy the life insurance should be considered if:

1.   The business owner is already an active participant in his or her own tax-qualified profit-sharing plan,

2.   Substantial assets are in the plan for more than two years,

3.   The business owner controls the business that sponsors the plan (the plan may have to be amended to permit the purchase of insurance).

Furthermore, Bob and Helen should consider second-to-die life insurance coverage as the most appropriate means to help pay their estate taxes because:

1.   It provides a death benefit at the precise time it is needed to help pay estate taxes at the second death.

2.   It's generally much more affordable than a life insurance policy of the same face amount insuring one life.

3.   A proper ownership strategy can help make the death benefit income tax-free and estate tax-free.

DEATH OF A BUSINESS OWNER

When a business owner dies, the cash needs of the owner's family are often at their highest. At the same time, the actual cash position of the owner's family may be at its lowest. Death doesn't stop the need for cash to meet next month's payroll, provide business working capital, pay suppliers and creditors, retain and replace key employees, and provide the owner's family with the income it needs to survive.

In addition, the death of a business owner often creates new cash needs, for example, (1) to pay estate and income taxes on pension distributions, (2) to pay estate taxes on existing business interests, or (3) to purchase the shares of a deceased shareholder under a written buy-and-sell agreement. Paying estate taxes can be the biggest problem because marginal rates can reach 55%.

Not only can family cash needs increase when a business owner dies, but traditional sources of cash can often dry up. Bankers are less likely to extend long-term credit for working capital, and suppliers are less likely to extend short-term credit to purchase inventory. All of this takes place in a business environment where customers are bargaining harder and harder for better prices and competitors are trying harder and harder to undercut competitors' prices and take away market share.

If a family is committed to keeping the family business in the family, it must accept the fact that the death of a senior family member may be the most critical point in the business's financial life. If the family is not prepared to deal with this, the business can easily fail. That's why family businesses are often called the most valuable and vulnerable asset of the family.

WHAT DOES THIS HAVE TO DO WITH RETIREMENT PLANNING?

Traditionally, business owners accumulate large pension and profit-sharing plan balances. However, with the potential of a 40% income tax, a 55% estate tax, and state income or inheritance taxes, the "shelter" provided by these plans can turn into a tax trap when the plan participant dies. Beneficiaries can face marginal total tax rates on pension distributions well over 60% at death (see Chapter 14). To help pay this potential tax, a plan participant can shift his or her plan asset structure so that premiums can be paid for life insurance.

By including life insurance in a qualified plan, a business owner is able to shift a nondeductible personal expense to the business, which can pay for it as part of a deductible pension contribution. Simply put, if the annual premium of a hypothetical $1,000,000 life insurance policy is $30,000 and the business owner is in a 40% marginal federal and state income tax bracket, she or he would save almost $12,000 a year in taxes by allowing the profit-sharing plan to pay for the insurance. The plan participant must only report as income the current cost of the life insurance protection received each year (roughly equal to the term insurance cost).

IRS rules set out the method of calculating the income tax on the insurance benefit. The participant's taxable income is determined by applying a one-year term premium rate (at the participant's current age) to the difference between the face amount of the policy and its cash surrender value. When there are two people insured, e.g., with second-to-die coverage, the one-year term premium rate is at the joint ages of the participant and second insured. There is a standard table to determine his tax. For second-to-die policies, the reportable income is very small. For example, for $1,000,000 of insurance, the amount reportable as income and the tax would be:[1]

	Total Income	Income Tax at 40%
Male and female, age 55	$ 190	$ 76
Male and female, age 65	$1,020	$ 408

HOW MUCH INSURANCE COVERAGE CAN BE PURCHASED?

Ordinarily, the amount of life insurance that can be purchased by a qualified pension or profit-sharing plan and paid to a beneficiary at the participant's death must be "incidental" to the plan's primary purpose of providing retirement benefits. For defined benefit plans, determining whether insurance is an incidental benefit requires comparing the insurance benefits provided by the plan with the retirement benefits provided by the plan. In general, insurance benefits may not exceed 100 times the participant's projected monthly retirement benefit in a defined benefit plan. Thus, if a business owner's expected retirement benefit is $10,000 per month, a defined benefit plan could purchase $1,000,000 of life insurance on his life without violating the incidental benefit rules. However, if the plan permits, additional life insurance can be provided pursuant to Rev. Rul. 74–307. This ruling allows insured death benefit in excess of 100 times the monthly retirement benefit for older plan participants.

For defined contribution plans, e.g., a profit-sharing plan, the test is based on contributions, not benefits. Usually, in order for term insurance (or universal life insurance) to be considered incidental in a defined contribution plan, annual premiums may not exceed 25% of the cumulative "annual additions" made to the employee's account. For traditional whole life insurance, premiums must be less than 50% of cumulative annual additions. This

---

[1]Rates based on U.S. Table 38, issued by the Treasury Department.

gives the business owner a great deal of flexibility in designing an appropriate insurance program for the qualified plan.

In addition to being able to pay premiums with pretax dollars, insurance funding rules for profit-sharing plans are more flexible than for most other qualified plans. Regardless of the incidental benefit rule, in a profit-sharing plan, funds that have been in the plan for at least five years can be used *entirely* toward the purchase of life insurance, without limitation (see Rev. Rul. 61–164 and Rev. Rul. 60–83). If plan funds are more than two years old, arguably up to 100% of those funds can also be used to purchase life insurance.[2] At this point, let's revisit Bob and Helen Goodie.

PAYING ESTATE TAXES WITH LIFE INSURANCE

In an estate planning seminar, Bob and Helen learned that if a second-to-die policy on their lives is owned outside of their estate by, for example, adult children or an irrevocable trust, the insurance can be paid estate tax-free. At Bob and Helen's death, the children or a trust for their benefit could use the insurance proceeds to purchase assets from Bob and Helen's estate.

The assets selected for purchase might be the most valuable assets of their estate, like family heirlooms, or those that are hardest to sell, like a family business. The cash received by their estate could then be used toward paying their estate taxes. Bob and Helen also learned that life insurance on the life of a plan participant that is owned by the participant's profit-sharing account is included in the participant's taxable estate. The effect of estate taxation is shown in Table 15-1.

TABLE 15-1

Potential Estate Taxation of Life Insurance

	Insurance out of Estate	Insurance in Estate
Death benefit paid	$1,500,000	$1,500,000
Potential estate tax bracket	0%	55%
After-tax cash available	$ 1,500,000	$ 675,000

---

[2]Despite these liberal rules, individuals may not want to use most of their profit sharing account to pay for life insurance premiums unless their insurance needs are more important than their retirement needs.

For Bob and Helen, Table 15-1 indicates how critical it is for their insurance to be paid estate tax-free. In a more subtle way, it also indicates how critical it is to use second-to-die life insurance to help pay their estate taxes. If Bob and Helen have tax-efficient wills and own their property correctly, no estate taxes should be due when the first of them dies. It's only at the surviving spouse's death that estate taxes will be due, and that's when the second-to-die death benefit must be paid estate tax-free.

When second-to-die insurance is owned and paid for by a profit-sharing plan, the first death is the signal to remove the policy from the plan and transfer it out of the surviving insured's estate.

When this is done correctly and in a timely manner, the life insurance will be paid income tax-free and estate tax-free when the surviving spouse dies. The technique of moving a policy out of the profit-sharing plan is called an "exit strategy," and, as we will soon see, four different exit strategies must exist in order to take into account all possible planning contingencies.

PLAN IMPLEMENTATION

Once Bob and Helen have made their decision to purchase a second-to-die policy in their profit-sharing plan, implementation is relatively simple. Bob should follow these four steps:

Step 1

Bob's profit-sharing plan should be amended, if necessary, to include a provision that permits participants in the plan the right to decide whether to purchase life insurance in their separate profit-sharing plan accounts. This is accomplished by allowing plan participants to actually direct the trustee of the profit-sharing plan—probably Bob—to purchase insurance. All employees must be eligible to take advantage of this option. Under pension nondiscrimination rules, if this option is not given to all employees, then the profit-sharing plan can buy insurance only if it is purchased for every participant in the plan.

Step 2

Bob directs the plan trustee to purchase a $1,500,000 second-to-die policy on himself and Helen. This is the appropriate amount that they need to help pay their income and estate taxes at the death of the surviving spouse. Bob and Helen must each take physical examinations and comply with the insurance company's underwriting requirements. The policy is purchased by the plan, and all premiums are paid by the plan from Bob's profit-sharing plan account, i.e., with before-tax dollars.[3] Premiums can be paid with existing funds in the plan and/or with employer contributions. The plan simply writes a check to the insurance company for the annual premium.

Step 3

As with any life insurance owned by a qualified plan, the value of the pure insurance benefit (death benefit less cash value) is taxed to the participant as ordinary income on an annual basis. For example, if Bob and Helen (ages 52 and 50, respectively) purchased a $1,500,000 second-to-die policy, the taxable income at their ages (Table 38 rate[*]) is about $165.00. This amount will increase each year as Bob and Helen get older because the imputed tax rate is based on age.

Step 4

Bob names the profit-sharing plan as beneficiary of the second-to-die policy. Bob creates his own personal beneficiary designation and files it with the plan trustee. The personal beneficiary designation controls what happens when one of the following four eventualities occur(s):

---

[3]At the time of this writing, the IRS has indicated concern about the propriety of allowing profit-sharing plans to purchase survivorship life insurance unless both insureds are plan participants. Before utilizing this strategy, the reader should consult with his or her own advisor.

[*]Based on government rates from U.S. Table 38.

1.   Bob dies first.
2.   Bob and Helen die in a common disaster.
3.   Helen dies first.
4.   Bob retires first.

For each of these contingencies, a set of directions exists within Bob's beneficiary designation. These directions explain what should be done with the insurance policy to make sure that at the second death, the pure insurance benefit (death proceeds less cash value) is paid estate tax-free to the children or a trust for their benefit.

Contingency 1: Bob Dies First

If Bob dies first, the death benefit of the second-to-die policy is not yet paid. But if left in the plan until Helen's death, it would be taxed in her estate since Helen is the beneficiary of Bob's profit-sharing account, which includes the insurance policy. Therefore, after Bob dies, the policy must be moved out of the profit-sharing plan into the hands of the children or to an already established irrevocable trust. If Bob and Helen were comfortable in letting their children own their policy after the first death, then Bob's beneficiary designation would state that at his death the policy should be distributed from the plan to their children, as joint owners. The children would then name themselves as equal beneficiaries. If Bob and Helen do not feel comfortable in letting their children own the policy, then it would be distributed to an already established irrevocable trust, which would name itself as beneficiary. Let's continue with the example, assuming that Bob and Helen trust their children.

At Bob's death, traditional planning would call for Bob's profit-sharing plan account to be distributed to Helen. In order to avoid income tax, Helen would then roll over this distribution into an IRA. Estate taxes on these funds would be avoided as a result of the unlimited marital deduction. This deduction allows every married person the opportunity to pass as much property as desired to his or her surviving spouse at death, estate tax-free, as long as the surviving spouse is a U.S. citizen.

The amount distributed to Helen would exclude the cash value of the second-to-die policy. The cash value would be distributed to the children as part of the policy, and they would report its value as a taxable pension distribution. To pay this tax and avoid any out-of-pocket outlay, the children could borrow[4] from the cash value of the policy an amount equal to the income tax due. The cash value of the policy would be part of Bob's taxable estate. However, no estate tax would be due unless the cash value of the policy exceeded the applicable unified credit exemption (which is $625,000 in 1998). This is the threshold amount below which no federal estate tax is due. Under IRS rules the children would receive an income tax deduction for any estate tax paid by Bob's estate on the cash value. Finally, future premiums on the second-to-die policy, if any, would be paid by the children through gifts made to them by Helen. The source of these gifts could be future distributions from Helen's new rollover IRA.

Contingency 2: Bob and Helen Die in a Common Disaster

The exit strategy for a common disaster is identical to the one for Bob dying first. If Bob and Helen die under circumstances in which the order of deaths cannot be determined, Bob's beneficiary designation would presume that he died first. Then, the second-to-die policy could be distributed from the plan to the children and the death proceeds paid to them. In this way, the pure death benefit would be removed from Bob and Helen's taxable estate. Only the cash value of the policy would be included in Bob's estate. However, this amount would be sheltered from estate tax by the applicable unified credit exemption.

Tax Summary—Contingencies 1 and 2

Federal Estate Tax. The cash value of the second-to-die policy will be included in Bob's gross estate. To the extent it is paid as part of the policy to the children, it will be subject to an estate tax. However, this tax can be sheltered by the federal unified credit exemption, which will increase from $625,000 in 1998 to $1,000,000 by 2006 and years thereafter. At the second death, the death proceeds of the insurance are paid to the children tax-free. There is no estate inclusion because the policy was distributed to

---

[4]Loans reduce the death benefit and require payment of interest.

the children or their trust and not gifted by the insured. A gift would invoke the three-year in contemplation of death rule.[5]

Federal Income Tax. When distributed from Bob's profit-sharing plan, the cash value of the second-to-die policy will be considered a taxable distribution for income tax purposes and will be subject to income tax. The children (or trust) will receive an income tax deduction for any estate tax paid by Bob's estate on that income (should there be any).

Contingencies 3 and 4: Helen Dies First or Bob Retires First

As you may have already guessed, the exit strategy for contingency 3 (Helen dies first) and contingency 4 (Bob retires first) are the same. If Helen dies first, Bob is the survivor, and to avoid estate taxes on the insurance, he must move the second-to-die policy out of his profit-sharing plan and out of his estate.

On the other hand, Bob might retire first. If he retires, Bob will roll over his profit-sharing plan balance into a personal IRA. Unfortunately, IRAs are not permitted to own life insurance. Therefore, Bob must also move the second-to-die policy out of the profit-sharing plan and out of his estate before rolling over his profit-sharing plan account to an IRA.

Bob has three alternative ways of moving his second-to-die policy out of his profit-sharing plan and out of his estate.

1. He can *withdraw* the policy from the profit-sharing plan and gift it to his children or to an already established irrevocable trust for his children's benefit.

2. He can *buy* the policy from the profit-sharing plan and gift it to his children or to an already established irrevocable trust for his children's benefit.

3. *Bob's children* can *buy* the policy directly from the profit-sharing plan.

From a tax perspective, alternative 3 is superior to alternatives 1 and 2, but each method has its merits, so, let's review them all.

---

[5]This rule says that if the insured gives a policy away and dies within three years of the gift, the death proceeds are generally included in his or her estate.

1. Bob Withdraws the Policy from the Plan and Makes a Gift. If Bob withdraws the second-to-die policy from the plan, its cash surrender value will be subject to personal income tax as a pension distribution. If Bob is under age 59½, a 10% penalty tax will be imposed in addition to the income tax. Bob can borrow on the cash surrender value of the policy to pay any taxes due.

Bob would then gift the policy to his children or to a trust for their benefit. The value of the policy for gift tax purposes could be reduced by any policy loan taken. The gift itself might be subject to a gift tax if its value were greater than the combined gift tax annual exclusions available at the time. In Bob's case, that would be $10,000 to each of his two children, or a total of $20,000. However, no gift tax should be paid as long as the taxable gift remains under the $625,000 (1998) federal unified credit exemption threshold for gift and estate taxes. Under IRC Section 2035, the death proceeds of the insurance will be out of Bob's estate if he survives three years.

2. Bob Buys the Policy from the Plan and Makes a Gift. Instead of withdrawing the policy from the plan, Bob can purchase the policy for its cash surrender value and gift it to his children or to a trust for their benefit. The purchase avoids the necessity of Bob having to pay income tax and penalty tax on the cash value of the policy. The policy is purchased from the plan, not distributed.

Nevertheless, as with the first alternative, there are potential gift taxes due when Bob gifts the policy to the children or to a trust. Taking a policy loan prior to the gift, however, can reduce the value of the policy for gift tax purposes. Also, the three-year rule of IRC Section 2035 still would apply. In this alternative, all cash paid by Bob to the profit-sharing plan to buy the insurance will come back to him in the form of a future retirement income.

3. Bob's Children Purchase the Policy from the Plan. This alternative can produce one of the most favorable tax results if the children (the buyers of the policy) are partners of both insureds in a valid partnership. The partnership could manage any family asset that would make it a valid partnership under state law. Removing the second-to-die policy by a bona fide sale would avoid the "transfer for value" rule, which makes all or part of the death proceeds of a life insurance policy, in excess of cost, income taxable when it is purchased ("transferred for a valuable consideration") by an impermissible party.

Certain purchasers of insurance policies, however, are permissible purchasers, and sales to them are not subject to this rule. They include: (1) a partner of the insured, (2) a partnership of which the insured is a partner, or (3) a corporation in which the insured is an officer or shareholder. As a partner, the children would qualify under exception (1).

In addition to qualifying as a permissible purchaser under the transfer for value rule, the children must also qualify as a permissible purchaser under the exception to the "prohibited transaction rules" created by the Department of Labor. Under these rules, children (but apparently not trusts) should be permitted, by exception, to buy insurance policies from their parents' qualified plans without the sale being considered a prohibited transaction.*

To summarize, Bob and Helen's children can implement this alternative (1) if they are partners with Bob and Helen in a valid partnership and (2) because they can be permissible purchasers under Department of Labor rules. A trust for the children's benefit apparently cannot implement this alternative because although it can be a partner of Bob and Helen in a valid partnership, it apparently is not a valid purchaser under Department of Labor rules.

There are a number of ways for the purchase of the policy to be arranged. One attractive way is for the children to give a promissory note for the reserve value of the policy to the plan as consideration for the sale. Then, as soon as they get the policy, they take a policy loan to repay most of the note. Since the note is larger than the amount that can be borrowed from the policy, the balance must be obtained either from Bob and Helen as a gift, from Bob's corporation as a bonus (to Rachel who works there), or simply from the children's individual funds.

This alternative has no income tax or penalty tax consequences because the policy is not removed from the plan as part

---

*The Department of Labor exception discussed above should be reviewed by an advisor before this strategy is considered.

of a pension distribution. Also, there would be no gift tax consequence because the policy is being purchased from the plan, and not gifted by Bob. Finally, there would be no potential estate inclusion issue either because in a sale there is no three-year wait to remove the insurance from the estate. The three-year problem only occurs when a policy is gifted to another by the insured.

In fact, the sale technique described above can also be implemented for contingencies 1 or 2 (if Bob dies first or if Bob and Helen die in a common disaster and it is presumed that Bob dies first). In either situation, the children still could buy the second-to-die policy from the profit-sharing plan before the death proceeds are paid at the second death. This would eliminate the income tax and potential excise tax cost to the children of receiving the second-to-die policy as a distribution from the plan. Ironically, the purchase price paid by the children for the policy would be received by the plan and ultimately rolled over by Helen into her own spousal IRA. It would also be distributed back to the children, plus growth, when Helen dies.

BENEFITS TO BOB AND HELEN

1. When both Bob and Helen die, the death proceeds of the second-to-die policy can be paid to their children estate and income tax-free.
2. Bob and Helen's estate taxes would be paid at a substantial discount, and their estate would be conserved for their children and grandchildren.
3. The software business would pass to Rachel, and after providing Helen with a life income, the profit-sharing plan would be distributed to all of Bob and Helen's children and grandchildren, especially to Aaron, who is a struggling musician and needs additional income.
4. The annual cost of the premiums paid is effectively reduced by Bob and Helen's marginal income tax bracket.
5. As the trustee of the profit-sharing plan, Bob would retain control of the insurance during his life in case his planning needs change.

LESSONS LEARNED

1. If properly owned, a second-to-die life insurance policy can help provide a family with the estate tax-free and income tax-free cash it needs to help fund the payment of estate taxes. It can also help pay the income taxes and possible excise taxes that may eventually be due on the qualified plan assets.

2. There is no restriction on the amount of profit-sharing assets that can be used to buy life insurance if the assets have been in the profit-sharing plan for more than five years, and only some restriction if plan assets are more than two years old (but less than five).

3. When a profit-sharing plan owns insurance, the premiums are paid with pretax dollars. This reduces or avoids the insured from using personal funds to pay premiums.

4. When a profit-sharing plan owns survivorship or second-to-die insurance, only a small economic benefit (measured by Table 38) is imputed as income to the insured. The older the insured is, the larger the economic benefit and the tax due.

5. Life insurance owned by an insured's profit-sharing plan account at death is included in the insured's gross estate. To avoid paying estate taxes, however, it is wise to buy second-to-die coverage so that an "exit strategy" can be implemented before the second death.

6. Exit strategies are designed to remove the insurance from the insured's estate before the death proceeds are actually payable (at the second death).

16

You Can't Take It with You: Business Succession Planning

PROFILE

Diamonds Are Forever, Inc., is a jewelry company owned equally by James and Penny. James is in charge of manufacturing and Penny is responsible for sales. James and Penny make a good team; they get along well as business partners, work hard, and really know their jobs.

James and Penny's hard work has paid off over the past several years. The company has increased income each year as the business continues to grow. They have contributed to the company's profit-sharing plan every year for the last 10 years. Currently, their corporation has been valued at $1,000,000.

BUSINESS CONTINUATION

During a recent meeting with their attorney and life insurance professional, the subject of business succession and continuation came up. This discussion focused on the impact of James's or Penny's death on the business and their respective families. It was a subject no one wanted to discuss, but it was critical to both of them.

The partners decided to enter into a buy-sell agreement to help protect the two owners and their respective families. This is a contract that obligates one shareholder to purchase the other's

stock in the company upon death, permanent disability, retirement, or other contingency. James and Penny agreed that the
purchase price for each shareholder's interest will be $500,000.
In the event James or Penny dies, the buy-sell agreement provides benefits to both the decedent's family and the surviving
shareholder (see Figure 16-1).

In short, a buy-sell program can:

- Protect the decedent's family by requiring the estate to
  sell the business interest for $500,000. The family
  receives cash instead of an interest in a closely held
  company that might be difficult to sell or generate
  income. The purchase price is income tax-free because
  the estate's cost basis in the business is stepped up to
  equal the purchase price, so gain is not realized. In other
  words, the estate sells the decedent's business interest
  for $500,000 and for tax purposes, because its cost basis
  is $500,000, no gain or profit is realized.

FIGURE 16-1

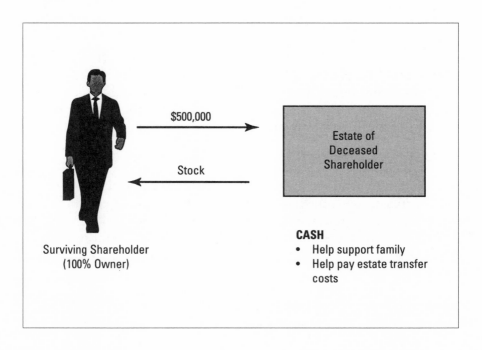

- Protect the company, because employees, lenders, customers, and suppliers will know that if one shareholder
  dies, the other will most likely continue the business.
- Establish the value of the company for federal estate tax
  purposes at $500,000 for each shareholder. This will
  help each family determine if there will be any federal
  estate tax liability due at the death of the shareholder.

An important benefit of a business succession agreement is
that the surviving shareholder knows that he or she will not have
to become a co-owner with the decedent's spouse, children, or other
beneficiary. As much as James and Penny respect each other and
their respective families, neither wants to become a co-owner with
a surviving spouse or child who knows little or nothing about the
business. The danger is that the surviving owner may do most or
all of the work and have to share income or profits with the other.

FUNDING PROBLEM

In order to create cash to help purchase a deceased shareholder's
interest upon death, James and Penny each want to purchase
$500,000 of life insurance. Penny will own and be the beneficiary
of the insurance on James's life and James will own and be the
beneficiary of the life insurance on Penny's life. Upon the death
of the first shareholder, the other will receive $500,000 of insur-
ance death proceeds tax-free. He or she can then use this money
to help purchase the decedent's shares of stock from his or her
estate (see Figure 16-2).

Unfortunately, the company and the shareholders have little
cash to pay life insurance premiums. Recently, the company purchased new equipment and expanded its office. It has substantial
debt that will be paid off in about five years. The parties, however, do not want to wait to purchase the insurance. They know
that premiums increase with age and there is a danger of becoming uninsurable or highly rated if health deteriorates. But they
simply do not have the cash flow to pay premiums for permanent
insurance on their lives. Without the insurance, the surviving
shareholder knows he or she would have a substantial financial
problem raising cash to purchase the stock. Simply put, James
and Penny know that neither of them could run the business and
pay off a $500,000 debt.

FIGURE 16-2

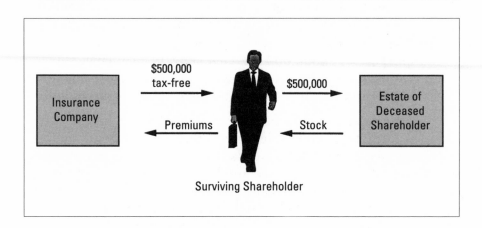

The parties considered purchasing term insurance. Term insurance is initially less expense than permanent insurance. But the premium for term increases and it can become very expensive to keep over time. In addition, some term policies lapse when the insured reaches a specific age. James and Penny have a permanent need for life insurance and want the benefits of permanent insurance.

FUNDING SOLUTION

Since the company has an established profit-sharing plan, the funds in James's and Penny's accounts can be used to purchase the needed life insurance. James would use his money to purchase a policy of life insurance on Penny's life for $500,000, and she would do the same for a policy on his life. (Note: In order for an existing profit-sharing plan to allow this type of purchase, it may have to be amended. In addition, the right to purchase insurance must be given to all plan participants.)

Qualified funds can be used to purchase life insurance as long as the premium cost is "incidental." Incidental refers to a limitation on the amount of money that can be spent on life insurance from existing funds in the plan or from employer contributions. The limitation makes sense because the primary purpose of a qualified plan is to accumulate money for retirement, not to

be done because Sam and Cybil need income, and the dividends on the Alpha stock would not be sufficient. When this occurs, the capital gains tax is not triggered. A CRT is a type of tax-exempt trust, because the ultimate beneficiary is a charitable organization. This means that the trustee would have $1,000,000 of cash to reinvest since no capital gains tax has to be paid at sale. If the trustee has more money to invest, more income can be generated for the donors: Sam and Cybil. Let's analyze trust income assuming the donors retain a 7% interest in the trust and the trustee earns a hypothetical interest rate of 7%. (See Table 19-2.)

Since the capital gains tax is avoided, Sam and Cybil can realize an income of $70,000 annually for life using the CRT, which is $12,600 more than they would have received had they sold their stock outside the CRT. Of course, the price they pay for this benefit is that they are making a deferred gift of trust principal to charity. Yet over their life expectancy of about 30 years, the CRT could generate $378,000 of additional income ($12,600 × 30).

WHICH TYPE OF CRT?

Sam decided that a unitrust would be best for him. He liked the idea that if trust principal increased in value, his income would increase. For example, suppose Sam created a 7% unitrust. If the trustee averaged a hypothetical return of 10%, which consisted of 7% income and 3% capital appreciation, the trust would be valued at $1,343,916 in 10 years. Sam's unitrust interest payment would then equal $94,074 (7% of $1,343,916).

Under the same set of circumstances, if Sam created a 7% charitable remainder annuity trust, he would only receive $70,000 annually. Excess earnings would be reinvested by the trustee and eventually benefit the ultimate charitable beneficiary. In the event

TABLE 19-2

CRT Income

Fair market value of donated stock	$1,000,000
Cash realized from sale of stock	1,000,000
Capital gains tax paid	0
Net amount to invest	1,000,000
Income for life @ 7%	70,000

income was insufficient, the trustee would have to invade trust principal.

INCOME TAX BENEFITS

Since a qualified charity is the ultimate beneficiary of the trust, the donor is entitled to an income tax deduction.

The value of the gift to charity is equal to the present value of the remainder interest of the trust. Since Sam and Cybil are unitrust income beneficiaries of the trust for life, the charity will not receive any trust principal until the surviving spouse dies. Using IRS tables, the charity's interest can be calculated so that Sam and Cybil know exactly how much they can deduct from their taxable income.

Assuming Sam and Cybil create a 7% unitrust and both donors are age 55, the present value of the gift to charity is equal to about $138,490. However, the maximum amount that can be deducted is 30% of Sam and Cybil's adjusted gross income. For example, if Sam and Cybil's adjusted gross income is $100,000, they could only use $30,000 of deductions in the first year. However, the unused portion can be carried forward for five years. This means that the unused deduction in the first years can be used in the next five successive years. The income tax deduction reduces tax liability and increases cash flow. Assuming Sam and Cybil are in a 35% income tax bracket, a $138,490 deduction equates to $48,472 in tax savings.

SUMMARY OF BENEFITS

A CRT can provide three significant benefits to Sam and Cybil. First, income is increased. Second, income tax liability is reduced by realizing a sizable deduction. Third, Sam and Cybil receive the personal benefit of providing a legacy to a worthy cause.

CONCERNS

There are two concerns in establishing a CRT. First, the donor must relinquish ownership of trust principal. Once the trust is funded with property, he cannot take it back. To set up a CRT, the donor should have other property, which may be needed for income or security.

The second concern involves children or other family members. When Sam and Cybil die, the charity gets the trust principal, not the children. If Sam and Cybil want to replace some or all of the property going to charity, they could purchase life insurance. The death benefit of the policy could be paid to the children. If properly owned, the proceeds would not be subject to estate tax or income tax. Sam and Cybil could pay premiums for the policy from trust income or from other sources of income, like the income tax savings from the charitable deduction.

TECHNICAL ISSUES

A CRT can be complicated. The following is a list of key issues that should be discussed before the trust is created:

KEY ISSUES

- Contributions to an annuity trust can only be made once—when the trust is established. If you want to make additional contributions, you would have to create another annuity trust. Additional contributions can be made to a CRUT.

- Some types of property may not be suitable for a CRT. For example, property encumbered with liens, certain types of businesses, or noncapital assets, such as an IRA, may not be appropriate. Check with your advisor.

- CRTs must provide a minimum payout to the noncharitable beneficiary of 5%. The maximum payout cannot exceed 50%.

- CRTs are better suited to "older" individuals, usually over age 50. This is because the present value of what the charity will receive in the future, usually after the donor's death, must exceed 10% of the value of the property contributed by the donor. Younger donors have longer life expectancies, which reduces the present value of the charity's future interest. It could easily fall below the 10% limitation.

- If property that is difficult to value is contributed to a CRT, a special trustee may be needed. This can occur if real estate or business interests are contributed to the trust.

- Avoid prearranged sales. The primary purpose of a CRT should be to help charity, not tax avoidance.

LESSONS LEARNED

1. Charitable plans can provide benefits to both the charity and the donor.
2. Individuals who have appreciated property which is needed for income may want to consider a charitable remainder trust (CRT).
3. There are two types of charitable remainder trusts, with important distinctions between the two.
4. If a CRT is used, be cognizant of key issues, and make sure children or other family members are not "disinherited."

APPENDIXES

A. A Spectrum of Retirement Plans for Businesses

B. Summary of Recent Legislation

C. Glossary of Terms

APPENDIX A

A Spectrum of Retirement Plans for Businesses

	PENSION AND PROFIT-SHARING PLANS	
	PROFIT SHARING	**MONEY PURCHASE**
BEST-SUITED FOR AN OWNER WHO...	• Is looking for flexibility to alter annual contributions (typically due to less stable cash flow). • Is highly compensated compared to rank-and-file. CONVENTIONAL • Is seeking simplicity in plan design and maintenance. • Particularly, younger principals. AGE BASED • Is relatively older than rank-and-file employees. • Is seeking to maximize his/her contribution while minimizing contributions for employees.	• Is willing to forego contribution flexibility for higher annual tax-deductible contributions than in a profit-sharing plan. • Is highly compensated compared to the rank-and-file. • Is seeking simplicity in plan design and maintenance. • Particularly, younger principals.
TAX-DEDUCTIBLE CONT-RIBUTIONS BY EMPLOYER	Discretionary each year.	Mandatory each year based on plan formula.
• ANNUAL MAXIMUM CONTRIBUTION	15% of participating payroll.	25% of participating payroll.
• SETTING CONTRIBUTION LEVELS	• Contribution level may be changed each year, at employer's discretion. • Contributions may be made regardless of profitability. • Plan must have a specific allocation formula that divides contributions among participants.	Contribution based on a formula in plan, usually a fixed percentage of compensation.
ANNUAL PARTICIPANT ALLOCATION/ BENEFIT LEVELS	Allocation maximum: 25% of individual participant's compensation, up to $30,000.	Allocation maximum: 25% of individual participant's compensation, up to $30,000.
INTEGRATION WITH SOCIAL SECURITY	Yes.	Yes.
PRE-TAX CONTRIBUTIONS BY EMPLOYEES	No.	No.
ELIGIBILITY/VESTING	• Minimum age and service requirements. • Employer can choose a vesting schedule if service requirement is one year or less.	• Minimum age and service requirements. • Employer can choose a vesting schedule if service requirement is one year or less.
REQUIREMENTS	• Annual reports. • Administration.	• Annual reports. • Administration.
DEADLINES	• Installation: Tax year-end. • Contributions: Due date of employer's tax return, including extensions.	• Installation: Tax year-end. • Contributions: Due date of employer's tax return, including extensions.***

PENSION AND PROFIT-SHARING PLANS

	TARGET BENEFIT	DEFINED BENEFIT
BEST-SUITED FOR AN OWNER WHO...	• Is relatively older than rank-and-file employees and is seeking high tax deductions while minimizing contributions for employees. • Is highly compensated compared to rank-and-file. • Has stable cash flow to meet annual funding requirements.	• Is 50 years or older with relatively younger rank-and-file employees. • Can benefit from the largest contributions possible. • Has stable cash flow to meet annual funding requirements. • Is willing to pay higher administrative costs.
TAX-DEDUCTIBLE CONTRIBUTIONS BY EMPLOYER	Mandatory each year based on plan formula.	Mandatory each year based on plan formula.*
• **ANNUAL MAXIMUM CONTRIBUTION**	25% of participating payroll.	No dollar limit, subject to funding limitations.**
• **SETTING CONTRIBUTION LEVELS**	• Contributions are actuarially determined dollar amounts for each participant, based on the plan's "target" benefit formula. • Contributions are not readjusted annually to reflect investment gains and losses.	• Contributions are actuarially determined dollar amounts, based on reaching plan's "defined" benefit for each participant. • Contributions are readjusted annually to reflect investment gains and losses and other factors.
ANNUAL PARTICIPANT ALLOCATION/ BENEFIT LEVELS	Allocation maximum: 25% of individual participant's compensation, up to $30,000.	Benefit limit: 100% of compensation to a maximum of $130,000 (as indexed for 1998).
INTEGRATION WITH SOCIAL SECURITY	Yes.	Yes.
PRE-TAX CONTRIBUTIONS BY EMPLOYEES	No.	No.
ELIGIBILITY/VESTING	• Minimum age and service requirements. • Employer can choose a vesting schedule if service requirement is one year or less.	• Minimum age and service requirements. • Employer can choose a vesting schedule if service requirement is one year or less.
REQUIREMENTS	• Annual reports. • Administration.	• Annual reports. • Administration. • Actuary required.
DEADLINES	• Installation: Tax year-end. • Contributions: Due date of employer's tax return, including extensions.***	• Installation: Tax year-end. • Contributions: Same as other pension plans, but with quarterly installments for some plans.***

* Defined benefit plan contributions are mandatory as required by actuarial determination; contributions may not be required in a given year if plan is fully funded or overfunded. ** Contributions cannot be more than the lesser of the amount actuarially required to provide the chosen benefit or the full funding limit. *** Contributions for money purchase, target benefit, and defined benefit plans must be made by 8 1/2 months after the close of the plan year, regardless of further extensions.

	401(k)	**SIMPLE 401(K) Savings Incentive Match Plan for Employees**
BEST-SUITED FOR AN OWNER WHO...	• Has a company with 25 or more employees. • Wants an employee benefit program that is inexpensive. • Is looking for a plan that allows pre-tax employee contributions.	• Has a company with no more than 100 employees receiving at least $5000 in compensation from the company for the preceeding year. • Wants an employee benefit program that is inexpensive and simple. • Is looking for a plan that allows pre-tax employee contributions. • Does not maintain any other qualified plan.
TAX-DEDUCTIBLE CONT-RIBUTIONS BY EMPLOYER	Discretionary each year.	Mandatory each year.
• **ANNUAL MAXIMUM CONTRIBUTION** • **SETTING CONTRIBUTION LEVELS**	15% of participating payroll (employee deferrals count toward the 15% maximum). • A special kind of profit-sharing plan that accepts deductible contributions from the employer and pre-tax contributions from the employee (employee contributions are called "deferrals"). • Flexible employer choices: No contributions, matching contributions, fixed contributions, and/or discretionary profit-sharing contributions, etc.	Greater of 1) 15% of payroll (including electric deferrals) or 2) $6000 per participant plus 3% of participants' compensation. • Employer may choose to make either: $1 for $1 matching contribution up to a limit of 3% of compensation for the full calendar year, OR a 2% non-elective contribution for each eligible employee who has received at least $5,000 (or lower, if employer elects) of compensation for the year. • No other contributions permitted.
ANNUAL PARTICIPANT ALLOCATION/ BENEFIT LEVELS	Allocation maximum: 25% of participant's compensation, up to $30,000 (includes employer contributions and participant deferrals).	Allocation maximum: 25% of individual participant's compensation, up to $30,000 (including employer contributions and participant's deferrals).
INTEGRATION WITH SOCIAL SECURITY	Employer's discretionary profit-sharing contributions may be integrated.	No.
PRE-TAX CONTRIBUTIONS BY EMPLOYEES	• Yes (called "deferrals"). • Annual maximum: 25% of each participant's compensation, up to $10,000 (indexed for 1998). • Deferrals by highly compensated employees are subject to non-discrimination test. • After-tax contributions also possible.	• Yes (called "deferrals"). • Annual maximum: 25% of each participant's compensation, up to $6,000 per participant (indexed for 1998) • No non-discrimination test for highly compensated employees.
ELIGIBILITY/VESTING	• Minimum age and service requirements. • Vesting schedule permitted for employer contributions if service requirement is one year or less (employee deferrals are always fully vested).	• Minimum age and service requirements. • All contributions are fully vested.
REQUIREMENTS	• Annual reports. • Involved administration.	• Simplified administration. • Annual reports.
DEADLINES	• Installation: Fiscal year-end. • Employer contributions: Due date of employer's tax return, including extensions. • Employee deferrals: 15th business day after the end of the month when deferrals were made.	• Installation: Prior to commencement of salary deferrals. • Employee deferrals: 15th business day after the end of the month when deferrals were made. • Employer contributions: Due date of employer's tax return, including extensions.

	Simple Saving Incentive Match Plan for Employees **SIMPLE IRA**	**SEP** Simplified Employee Pension
BEST-SUITED FOR AN OWNER WHO...	• Has a company with no more than 100 employees receiving at least $5000 in compensation from the company for the preceeding year. • Wants an employee benefit program that is inexpensive and simple. • Is looking for a plan that allows pre-tax employee contributions. • Does not maintain any other qualified plan.	• Has few or no employees. • Wants a plan that is simple and inexpensive to install and administer.
TAX-DEDUCTIBLE CONT-RIBUTIONS BY EMPLOYER	Mandatory each year.	Discretionary each year.
• **ANNUAL MAXIMUM DEFERRAL**	No specified limit.	15% of participating payroll (employee deferrals count toward the 15% maximum).
• **SETTING CONTRIBUTION LEVELS**	• Employer may choose $1 for $1 matching contribution up to a limit of 3% of compensation (may be as little as 1% in 2 out of 5 yrs.) OR a 2% non-elective contribution per eligible employee with at least $5,000**** of compensation. • No other contributions permitted. Contributions are made into an IRA for each employee.	• Employer determines deductible contributions each year. • Contributions are made into an IRA for each employee.
ANNUAL PARTICIPANT ALLOCATION/ BENEFIT LEVELS	No specified limit, but effectively $12,000.	Allocation maximum: lesser of 15% of participant's compensation, or $30,000 (includes employer contributions and participant deferrals).
INTEGRATION WITH SOCIAL SECURITY	No.	Yes.†
PRE-TAX CONTRIBUTIONS BY EMPLOYEES	• Yes (called "deferrals"). • Annual maximum: $6,000 (1998) • No non-discrimination test for highly compensated employees.	Only for SAR-SEP plans established prior to January 1, 1997.
ELIGIBILITY/VESTING	• Any employee who received $5,000 in compensation from the employer during any 2 prior calendar years and who is reasonably expected to receive at least $5,000 during the current calendar year must be eligible to participate. • All contributions are fully vested.	• Limited eligibility requirements: Any employee who is at least 21 years old and has performed "service" in at least 3 of the immediately preceding 5 years must be included.†† Employees whose total compensation for the year is less than $400 (as indexed for 1998) may be excluded. • 100% immediate vesting.
REQUIREMENTS	• Minimal administration. • No IRS filings.	• Minimal administration. • No IRS filings.
DEADLINES	• Installation: Prior to commencement of salary deferrals. • Employee deferrals: 30 days after end of month to which they relate. • Employer contributions: Due date of employer's tax return, including extensions.	• Installation: Due date of employer's tax return, including extensions. • Contributions: Due date of employer's tax return, including extensions.

† Integration with Social Security not permitted in IRS model SEP. †† Lower age and service if employer chooses.
**** or lower if employer elects.

Summary of Recent Legislation

1996 & 1997 LAWS CAN AFFECT YOUR RETIREMENT—KNOW THE RULES

In 1996 and 1997, Congress passed two important laws affecting retirement planning. The 1996 law is called "The Small Business Job Protection Act of 1996 (SBJPA). The 1997 law is called "The Taxpayers Relief Act." This chapter will summarize the most important aspects of the laws affecting your retirement planning options. The SBJPA pertains mostly to business owners who may want to start or amend a qualified retirement plan. The Taxpayer Relief Act is important to everyone.

THE SMALL BUSINESS JOB PROTECTION ACT OF 1996

SBJPA created two new types of plans for a business owner contemplating creating a retirement plan for his employees or amending an existing plan. The new plans are called SIMPLE IRA and SIMPLE 401(k). Unfortunately, because those plans are tax qualified and are variations of traditional types of retirement plans [simplified employee plans (SEPs) and 401(k)s], understanding them is not always "simple," although the intent of the law is to make these plans easier to establish and administer for a business owner.

Making Plans "Easy"

A 401(k) plan is an arrangement permitting eligible employees to contribute a percentage of their pretax salary to a retirement plan.

Generally, the maximum amount an employee can contribute is $10,000 (1998) not to exceed 25% of salary (which is the limit under section 415 of the Internal Revenue Code).

One difficulty with a 401(k) plan is determining who is a "highly compensated employee" and how much he or she can contribute. This is important to know because a 401(k) plan must satisfy a unique nondiscrimination test based on the amount of contributions (deferrals) made by employees called non-highly compensated (NHC) employees, compared to the contributions made by highly compensated employees (HCE). The purpose of the test is to insure that the benefits of the plan are being fairly used by both rank-and-file employees and highly compensated employees.

Under prior law, the definition of an HCE employee was complicated. The SBJPA simplified the definition to include, generally, any employee whose compensation from the employer in the prior year was $80,000 or more (indexed for inflation) or who is more than a 5% owner. Thus, most business owners, executives, and managers are classified as highly compensated.

Classification of all employees is critical because the next step is to calculate the actual deferral percentage of the HC employees and compare it to the actual deferral percentage of the NHC employees. As long as the HC employee percentage is within statutory limits, the plan passes the test. The statutory differential limit between the two groups of employees is generally 2%. To illustrate this comparison, let's look at an example. Suppose XYZ Corp. has 35 employees, five of whom are HC employees and the balance rank-and-file. Let's further assume that the average NHC employee contributes 3% of his or her salary to the 401(k) plan. The highly compensated employees can then contribute no more than 5% of salary on average to their 401(k) plan accounts.

In small companies (i.e., under 50 employees) the participation and contributions of rank-and-file employees to 401(k) plan accounts are extremely important. The lower the collective contribution by NHC employees, the lower the contribution that can be made by HC employees. To encourage participation and greater contributions by rank-and-file employees, management usually matches a portion of their contribution. Usually, a match encourages participation because it enhances the employee's retirement without cost to the employee.

Family Members' Aggregation Eliminated

Many family businesses that are owned and managed by one spouse may employ the other spouse. Under prior law, spouses were treated as one employee in determining the maximum amount that could be contributed or funded in a retirement plan. In effect, the prior law discriminated against spouses who worked for the same company, assuming one spouse is an HCE. To illustrate this type of "reverse" discrimination, let's look at an example.

Suppose Smith Widget Supply Company employs Diane and Jim Smith, (wife and husband). Each spouse earns a salary of $160,000 annually. For purposes of a qualified plan, their contribution would be limited as if they were one employee, e.g., $30,000 for defined contribution plan. But they would both share in that contribution.

For family-owned businesses employing spouses, the good news is that the 1996 Act eliminated family aggregation. This permits each spouse to be treated as any other employee entitled to the same contribution based on his or her reasonable compensation and classification. Thus, a smart retirement strategy for business owners, assuming it makes sense otherwise, is to employ their spouses on a full-time or even part-time basis, assuming the spouse provides services for his or her income. As long as the plan is drafted carefully, it can permit part-time employees to participate as long as no discrimination occurs.

Suppose, for example, that in Smith Widget Supply Diane works and runs the company on a full-time basis. Her husband, Jim, is the office manager but only works 15 hours per week and earns a salary of $25,000 per year. A plan could be drafted to permit Jim to participate. Of course, all part-time employees who work similar hours may also participate. The additional cost of contributing to other employees should also be considered.

Simplified Plans—"SIMPLE"

Beginning in 1997, certain employers have the option of creating a SIMPLE 401(k) plan or a SIMPLE IRA. Eligible employers are those who had 100 or fewer employees in the last calendar year and employees who received compensation of $5000 or more in the preceding two years and are expected to receive $5000 or more of compensation in the current year. In addition, the plan must limit deferrals to $6000 per year (which is indexed).

Once a SIMPLE plan is created, the employer must make contributions in the form of a match or in the form of an across-the-board nonelective contribution to all eligible employees. A SIMPLE IRA typically requires a dollar-for-dollar match on the first 3% of salary an employee contributes for the year. For example, if an employee contributes $3000 to the plan (which represents 3% of salary at $100,000) then the employer must contribute or match the same amount. As an alternative, in two out of any five years the employer can offer a match of less than 3%, but no less than 1%, if the employees are given proper and timely notice.

Instead of a match, an employer can make a 2% nonelective contribution to all eligible employees. Under this option, salary is capped at $160,000 (in 1998), so the maximum employer contribution that can be made to an employee in 1998 is $3200 (2% of $160,000).

The employee is always 100% vested in all contributions made by the employer. This means that if the employee terminates employment for any reason, he or she is entitled to all of the money in the account. It should be noted that for a business owner, the greater the participation and contributions made by employees to a SIMPLE plan, the greater the cost to the employer. This is the exact opposite of many types of traditional 401(k) plans, in which the employer wants the NHC employees to contribute and participate. That is because higher deferrals made by NHC employees can allow the deferrals by HC employees to be higher. Therefore, for some business owners, a SIMPLE plan might be simple to establish and maintain but more costly than a traditional 401(k) plan.

It should also be noted that a salary cap does not apply for matching purposes in a SIMPLE IRA. Thus, an employee earning $200,000 and contributing $6,000 is entitled to a $6,000 employer matching contribution (i.e., $12,000 total). In addition, and employee earning $6,000 can contribute $6,000 and receive a $180.00 match from the employer.

The second type of "simple" plan is a SIMPLE 401(k). The employer has the same matching or contribution obligation as described above. There are, however, some differences:

- Compensation is capped at $160,000 for all purposes (in 1998).

- There is no option to reduce the match, unlike a SIMPLE IRA.
- A SIMPLE 401(k) is subject to additional restrictions regarding the maximum amount contributed to an employee's account, generally called Section 415 limits.
- Form 5500 is required.
- Eligibility can be limited to one year of service and age 21 and 1000 hours.

Reduced Administration for SIMPLE Plans

The 1996 law regarding SIMPLE plans eliminated the need to satisfy actual deferral percentage and contribution tests that still exist in traditional 401(k) plans. In addition, the top-heavy rules which require minimum contributions for rank-and-file employees do not apply.

THE TAXPAYER RELIEF ACT OF 1997

The 1996 law changed the way *employers* can create retirement plans for employees. The 1997 law changed some of the ways *individuals* can accumulate money for retirement by expanding several IRAs.

Roth IRA

A Roth IRA (named after Senator Roth from Delaware) enables eligible individuals to contribute $2000 annually, less the amount contributed to a traditional IRA. A Roth IRA, however, is different from traditional IRAs in three important ways. First, contributions are nondeductible. Second, and most important, is that distributions are income tax-free, provided they are made to a person over the age of 59½ and who has maintained the IRA account for five or more years. Third, participation is not based on whether you or your spouse participate in an employer-sponsored qualified plan. Eligible participation is based solely on income. If you are married and filing a joint tax return, your contribution limits start to phase out if your adjusted gross income is $150,000.

A total phase-out of eligibility occurs for couples whose adjusted gross income is $160,000 or more. For single taxpayers, the phase-out begins at $95,000 and ends at $110,000 of adjusted gross income.

Distributions made before age 59½ or prior to the five-year holding period are subject to ordinary income tax, to the extent they exceed contributions not previously distributed, and a 10% tax penalty. The tax and penalty are waived if the five-year holding period requirement is satisfied and either the IRA holder dies and the account is paid to a beneficiary or the distribution is attributable to the IRA holder becoming totally disabled.

Taxpayers who are eligible to contribute to a Roth IRA or traditional IRA must decide which one is better. Remember, you can only contribute $2000 (or $4000 per couple) total to either type of IRA. Also remember that both types of IRAs require the taxpayer to have earned income to make a contribution.

IRA Comparison

In a traditional IRA, the contribution is income tax-deductible. When comparing the two IRAs, your income tax bracket at the time of contribution and at the time of retirement are important factors. For example, a person in a 28% income tax bracket saves $560.00 in taxes on a $2000 deductible IRA contribution. To adequately compare the two, this tax savings could be invested in a side fund. Let's compare the two using the following assumptions:

- $2000 is invested in a traditional IRA account and a Roth IRA each year for 25 years.
- Each account will grow tax-deferred at an assumed 8% rate.
- The income tax savings from the deductible IRA is to be invested in a hypothetical side fund which earns 8% annually pretax and 5.70% after tax.
- After 25 years, the retiree will liquidate his or her account.

The results are as follows:

Roth IRA

Future hypothetical value	$146,212
Income tax on distribution	0
Net amount	$146,212

Deductible IRA

Future hypothetical value	$146,212
Income tax @ 28%	40,939
Net amount	105,273
Hypothetical side fund value	
($560.00 @ 5.70% for 25 years)	29,705
Total amount	$134,978

The example above shows that individuals in modest income tax brackets may wind up with more money in a Roth IRA—which might be the smart move to make. However, to accurately compare the two strategies requires discipline. The taxpayer would have to actually invest the tax savings generated by the deductible IRA contribution. If you do not have that discipline, forgo the income tax deduction and purchase a ROTH IRA. You will have more money at retirement.

The deductible IRA might make the most sense for individuals currently in high income tax brackets who would be in lower brackets at retirement. To reduce your income tax bracket, you could take distributions over your life or over a number of years so that you don't have a large taxable distribution in one year. The key point and smart strategy is to realize that an income tax deduction is not always the most efficient option.

Rollover to Roth

If you own an IRA account, you may want to convert or roll over to a Roth IRA. The primary purpose of using this strategy is to convert taxable distributions into tax-free distributions. However, the conversion will cause you to pay income tax on the conversion (but not a penalty tax even if you are under age 59½).

If the conversion is completed in 1998, the taxable amount is ratably charged over a four-year period. This benefit can save you income taxes. Let's look at an example. Kathy is 45 years old and has $100,000 in her IRA account. If she elects to convert her

IRA into a Roth IRA, she will receive taxable income of $25,000 per year for four years. This income might not increase her marginal tax bracket. This, of course, assumes Kathy has the money to pay the additional income tax. If she converts, her Roth IRA grows income tax-deferred, and when she reaches age 59½, she can take income tax-free distributions. Depending on the circumstances, the income tax-free withdrawals can more than offset the income tax that she pays at the time of conversion.

The conversion to a Roth IRA is not available to everyone. Taxpayers with adjusted gross income in excess of $100,000 do not qualify. However, some individuals may be able to control income by deferring salary or bonus. For those who have that option, it might be smart to reduce income to qualify for the conversion and convert an IRA to a Roth IRA. After all, having income tax-free money later in life should make retirement more enjoyable.

Increase in Exclusion from Gain on the Sale of a Personal Residence

The Taxpayer Relief Act of 1997 increased the amount of gain you can exclude when you sell your principal residence. Now, married taxpayers, regardless of age, filing a joint tax return can exclude $500,000 from gain on the sale of a home. For single taxpayers, the excluded gain is $250,000.

The only requirements are:

1. The home must be your principal residence.
2. You have to have lived there two out of the five years prior to the sale. (Multiple sales and exclusions are therefore possible as long as the time requirements are met.)

To determine the gain upon sale, you take your sales price and reduce it by your cost basis and other expenses incurred in selling, such as broker fees, legal fees, advertising, and other similar costs. Your cost basis includes what you paid for the home and all of your improvements. To prove your cost basis, keep records of your improvements. In general, improvements include major work like extensions and installation of major utilities, central air conditioning and heating systems, for example.

SOUTHEASTERN COMMUNITY COLLEGE LIBRARY

3 3255 00066 9292

HG 179 .P5552 1999
Plan smart, retire rich :

SOUTHEASTERN COMMUNITY
COLLEGE LIBRARY
WHITEVILLE, NC 28472